SOME OTHER SON

Some Other Son

STEVE COX

Copyright 2017. All rights reserved
by Steve Cox
The names of some individuals in the story have been
changed for privacy purposes.

TABLE OF CONTENTS

Preface	1
Chapter 1	3
Chapter 2	0
Chapter 3	0
Chapter 4	0
Chapter 5	0
Chapter 6	0
Chapter 7	0
Chapter 8	0
Chapter 9	0
Chapter 10	0
Chapter 11	0
Chapter 12	0
Chapter 13	0
Chapter 14	0
Chapter 15	0

PREFACE

The following statistics highlight the state of the foster care system. Children in the system, who for no cause of their own, are at risk of becoming drug addicts, criminals, homeless and burdens on society for the rest of their lives. The challenges faced by them will shape their destiny.

In 2014, 22,392 youth emancipated—or "age-out"—from the foster care system when they reach age 18 or finish high school. (Some states have extended care through the ages of 20 or 21.) Youth in foster care often do not get the help they need with high school completion, employment, accessing health care, continued educational opportunities, housing and transitional living arrangements. Studies of youth who have left foster care have shown they are more likely than those in the general population to not finish high school, be unemployed, and be dependent on public assistance.

Many find themselves in prison, homeless, or parents at an early age.[1]

In 2012 there were 3.3 million reports of violence against children resulting in 251,764 placements in the foster care system. The 'system' promised to give them a better life with a family, a home and safety. That year 23,439 aged-out of foster care. In other words, they were never reunited with their families. Statistically, of those who age-out, one-in-five will become homeless, only half will be employed at age 24, less than three percent will earn a college degree, seventy-one percent of the women will become pregnant by age 21, and one-in-four will experience PTSD.[2]

Joe Parker was a foster child who almost fell into the abyss. His story is unique in many ways. He beat the odds and pulled himself up and out with his never-quit attitude and positive outlook. Joe's intention, and the author's desire, is for his story to be a source if inspiration for the youth who are in the foster care system today.

The events in this story are true, but some of the names have been changed in the interest of privacy.

—§—

1. Source: Adoption and Foster Care Analysis and Reporting System (AFCARS) FY 2014 data
2. Jim Casey Youth Opportunities Initiative

CHAPTER 1

THE ambulance driver sped through town faster than he normally did. Subconsciously, the foot pressure he applied to the gas pedal was proportional to the urgency of his mission. His training as a first-responder tempered the panic he might otherwise have felt for the passenger strapped to the gurney in the back of his emergency vehicle. Nonetheless, he raced the boxy vehicle, with lights and siren blaring, around corners and over potholes on the edge of recklessness to accomplish his mission. Time was of the essence.

In the back of the ambulance was Nancy Parker. Until today she was a 27 year old beauty, a petite and attractive brunette. As a married mother of one stepson, her only mistake in life was the rekindling of the crush she had once had on Dicky Carrigan back in high school. It would become a mistake so big, that it altered her life forever, and the lives of many others.

Years before this horrible day, Nancy and Carrigan had attended high school in working-class town in north central Massachusetts. Back then, Carrigan was known around campus as a high school bully. He used his stocky, muscular build to intimidate anyone who got in his way.

He thought of himself as a ladies' man. Nancy and he met in high school and began dating frequently. She had a quintessential school girl crush on him. He was good looking and people treated him with respect. If they didn't, they might get smacked around. Not many of the other students dared challenge him, lest they suffer the consequences. Carrigan never lost a fight. He didn't always win, but he never lost. Anyone who challenged him would end up regretting it. Not many students liked him, but they all feared and respected him.

Nancy was his girlfriend, his steady. Or at least she thought she was. Most others also thought she was. The rumors began to circulate when classmates noticed Carrigan paying attention to some of the other coed beauties. The whispers started when he was seen hanging around some other gals' lockers, or giving them flirtatious grins from across the classroom.

It fueled his ego that there were three teenage girls, including Nancy, who were eager recipients of his attention. At first, none of the three were aware that he was playing around with other gals in school, and Carrigan wanted to keep it that way. They each

CHAPTER 1

thought they were his 'steady'. The exclusive arm candy of the class bully. The big man on campus.

Secrets aren't secrets for very long in the halls of a typical high school, and this was a typical high school. All three ladies became the subject of rumors and smirking glances. As Nancy strolled down the hallway between classes, she heard the snickers. Something was up.

In the privacy of the girls room, her best girlfriend, Jill, told her what was up, "Carrigan is cheating on you." The news caught her off-guard. Nancy became flooded with emotions. She was crushed to the point of tears. Jill tried to soften the blow with, "He's a jerk anyway." But Nancy was inconsolable.

As the reality sunk in, she became angry at Carrigan, angry at the other girls, and embarrassed that she was the hot topic du jour of the rumor mill. On one side she wanted to confront his other two girlfriends. On the other side wanted she to break up with Carrigan. At the same time she was worried about how he'd react. He'd often take out his anger by pounding his fist on a wall, or the face of someone smaller than he. Nancy did not want to be the recipient of his anger. He was the one who hurt her emotionally, and now she worried that he'd harm her physically.

In those days, social media was not at the speed of the Internet, but mouth-to-ear rumors were almost as fast. Nancy learned who the two other girls were, and that they were as equally crushed by Carrigan's philandering. She did not know them personally, but she knew who they were. Carrigan had been careful not to date within the same social circles, hoping that the soft isolation between cliques would shade his deception.

One of the other objects of his affection was Roberta Grant. She was also a good looking petite brunette. In all appearances she was very similar to Nancy. Through the messenger service provided by mutual friends, the three forlorn ladies arranged to meet after school, in a corner of the parking lot. A spot that was out of sight from anyone who might be peering out of a classroom window. It also provided a good lookout. A vantage point to surveil their surroundings. They didn't want Carrigan to know that they knew about each other.

In the parking lot that sunny afternoon, the three met to compare notes. Their anger was not cast upon one another, but toward that school bully, Carrigan. They all agreed that they would each break up with the bastard. He had been caught and they were not going to be his playthings any longer. Together, they formed a plan.

The next day, Nancy asked Carrigan to meet her in the parking lot after school. At the same spot where the girls had met the day before. She used the ruse that she had a surprise for him. Indeed she did. The other two gals would be waiting close by, out of sight, hidden in a parked car. The plan was for all three to confront him at the same time.

CHAPTER 1

They all understood that there would be safety in numbers. If Carrigan became angry, three against one would be a more even match. They could protect one another and bear witness if he reacted violently.

Three of them together also made it safer for another purpose. There was no doubt in their minds that Carrigan was a scoundrel, but subconsciously, the ladies weren't sure they could trust one another. If they confronted Carrigan individually, one of them might have convinced Carrigan to dump the other two and stay with her. Carrigan would surely agree to such an arrangement, otherwise he was going to lose all three.

The three gals waited in the dark corner of the parking lot, two in a car and Nancy in plain sight. She quietly paced a few steps back and forth while occasionally steeling a reassuring glance from the heads carefully peering above the back seat of a parked car.

The designated rendezvous time came and went. Tensions increased while the three continued to wait. It was common behavior for Carrigan to make someone wait for him. It was just another way to insert his control. Twenty minutes late, Nancy spotted Carrigan swaggering toward her from the back door of the school building.

Her senses alerted and her heart started to pound. The anticipation was almost too much for her. Her thoughts reeled. *What would Carrigan do?*

How would he react? At least there were three of us against the one of him.

Nancy did her best to feign a smile as he approached. When Carrigan was only a few yards away. She signaled to the gals in the car with the hand signal they were waiting for. They swung both back doors open and stepped out of the car. Carrigan didn't pay much attention to the two people getting out of a car nearby. As far as he knew, they were just somebody having a smoke in the parking lot. Then he recognized them.

He stopped in his tracks a few feet from the threesome. His happy expression turned to pursed eyebrows then to anger as he hesitated for a moment to read the situation. It took only a few seconds for the event to gather meaning. He had been caught. These ladies were not here to stroke his ego and tell him how wonderful he was.

Slowly, he shook his head from side to side with a look of disgust on his face. Without saying a word, he turned around and began walking back toward the door he had emerged from.

When the door closed behind him, the three ladies smiled and high-fived each other. Relieved that an ugly confrontation had been averted, yet disappointed that they weren't afforded the opportunity to vent their anger. Once again, Carrigan was in control. He made them wait, and he refused to be bullied by the three young woman.

CHAPTER 1

Secretly, they each still coveted the thought of being his exclusive girlfriend. There was something about him that they still desired. Was it the respect they garnered by being the girlfriend of the class bully? Was it a physical attraction? Long after that day they each still craved his attention.

Time passed, and for many years he remained in Nancy's thoughts. Even during her marriage to another man, her desire for Carrigan never waned.

A decade later she was now a woman with a husband and a young stepson and a career. Yet there was something about those days with Carrigan she couldn't get out of her mind. The memories of his cruel bullying had faded with time, and reminiscence of the way she felt back then filled her with a wistful desire to feel his compassion.

After graduation, Nancy had found a job at a chemical company nearby. Over time, she had worked her way up in the accounting department. Her career received a boost and a promotion when she discovered a one hundred thousand dollar accounting error that fell in favor of her employer. Her young life was off to a good start.

Nancy married Brian Parker in 1973. Brian had a three year old son from a previous marriage. He was in active duty military service and was often away from home. When Brian wasn't in town, her loneliness and memories of the past lead her to re-establish contact with Carrigan. They met and began to secretly see each other when circumstances allowed it. It developed into a passionate affair. Her loneliness was fulfilled by her old fling from high school. One thing led to another and she became pregnant by Carrigan. Not wanting to abort the child, she let Brian believe it was his.

Carrigan wanted the secret to be kept as well. He had married Roberta Grant, the one-time jilted lover from high school. She was the one gal of the three high school beauties who managed to win back his affection.

After returning home from military duty, Brian intercepted some phone calls and messages from Carrigan. It didn't take him long to figure out what was going on. His wife was having an affair. He wasn't happy about it. In an attempt to rescue his marriage, he decided to confront Carrigan.

In those days, Carrigan was known to hang out at the Paddock Lounge, a local watering hole. Brian decided to look for him where he knew he'd be.

Brian took a seat in a dark corner of the lounge and waited. As expected Carrigan appeared, sat at the bar and ordered a beer. When Carrigan walked into the men's room, Brian followed close behind. This was his opportunity to demand that Carrigan, "Stay away from my wife." The bully, Carrigan, never liked being told what to do and the two started throwing punches. To rub salt in the wound, Carrigan yelled at Brian, "She's pregnant with my kid. It's mine, not yours."

CHAPTER 1

A few weeks after the incident at the Paddock, Brian had to leave town on another military assignment. After a day of drinking at the Paddock Lounge, Carrigan took the opportunity to visit his very pregnant, secret lover at her house. He had tried to keep his affair with Nancy a secret, only telling a few drinking buddies. Carrigan's wife, RobertaF, had not yet learned of his affair with Nancy and he wanted to keep it that way.

In Nancy's house, their discussion turned into anger. The anger turned into violence as Carrigan flew into a drunken rage. He punched her in the stomach and beat her face to an unrecognizable broken bloody mess. He beat and kicked the petite Nancy, hoping that she's lose the baby, his baby. Afterward, he threw her down the stairs.

Now Nancy was in the back of the ambulance, a bloodied face, bruised body, broken bones and almost 9 months pregnant. She was carrying a child he wanted no part of.

The ambulance driver hurriedly wheeled her into the emergency room where doctors were already expecting them. His job accomplished, he left on another call.

The doctors went right to work trying to save the life of both Nancy and her unborn child.

The next day, Nancy woke to the aches and pains of a battered body. Her arms and legs hurt when she moved them, her face felt sore and swollen. A mirror on the wall reflected the face of a woman she didn't recognize. That woman looked back at her with battered black eyes, cracked lips and cuts on her forehead and cheeks.

Groggy and confused, full panic set in when she realized that the mound in her stomach was missing. Her baby was gone. Sobbing uncontrollably, she thought that Carrigan had succeeded in his despicable mission.

After a few days of recovery of her physical being, Nancy was moved to a psychiatric ward. She still had a swollen and bruised face, a few broken bones, and no baby in her womb. It was the beginning of her life in mental institutions, homelessness, and the occasional lucidity that came in short durations.

The nursing staff tried to assure Nancy that the son who was cut from her womb was healthy and safe, but it had little effect. The damage was done. She was barely capable of understanding all that had happened.

The physical trauma of the beating almost killed her. And being near full-term pregnant, she was not capable of defending herself or escaping his wrath. She was helpless.

The beating from Carrigan left her with severe psychological damage. The physical wounds would heal with time, but the deep mental scars were permanent.

Meanwhile, baby Joe slept quietly in the hospital nursery, unharmed and unaware. His life would not be an easy one.

CHAPTER 2

Joe's life began in north central Massachusetts. In a small town called Leominster. From the start, his very existence was challenged by the turmoil in the lives of the man and woman who brought him into this world. It wasn't known to him that the very man who gave him life was also the cause of the future struggles and vicissitudes in his life. Joe would learn life's hard lessons early on. The comforts that most of us take for granted as children, a safe home, a loving mother and father, were only dreams for Joe.

As a small child, he lived for a while with grandmother Mem, his mother's mother. His biological mom could not manage traditional motherhood duties because of her severe mental health problems. She would have liked to be his mom, but the demons in her psyche held her distant, both physically and emotionally.

His earliest memories of her are of the times when he and Mem visited her in a hospital. She was behind a door with a window. There was a slot in the door at his eye level big enough for her meals to be passed through. Joe was just tall enough to see her and talk with her through that opening. Physical contact, the warm and loving type between mother and son, was strictly prohibited. Ironically, physical contact may have been good medicine for both.

At his young age he didn't understand why she lived like this. He'd ask Mem, "Why is she here? Why does she act like that?" It wasn't until he was about 9 years old that he began to realize that something was wrong with her. He was then old enough to comprehend that she was not well; that she had an illness that many people did not understand, including himself. Yet even at his young age, he understood that the things that she did, and the words that she spoke were not her fault. Her actions were unintentional.

There was meaning behind Mem's explanation, "She is sick." To understand mental illness at his young age would sow the seeds of some future pursuits in Joe's life. His Mom didn't act like a normal person, and had to be kept separate from him and others. Even so, she was his mother and he craved her love, her touch, and her reassurances.

Growing up, Joe never knew who his father was. Joe was told that his dad departed when Joe was too young to form any meaningful memories of him.

CHAPTER 2

There was, however, a male figure in Joe's early life. He remembers sitting on the lap of a large man in his grandmother, Mem's, kitchen. In the eyes of a three year old, any man is a big creature. This man had very large hands and the warmth of his body was comforting. In those memories, Mem was cooking and making Rice Krispy treats. Joe remembers Mem handing the treats to the big man who in turn fed them to Joe. This man would show up at random times in Mem's kitchen. At that young age, Joe didn't even know what an uncle was, but Mem told him that the big man, Carrigan, was his uncle.

Around town Carrigan was know as a likable guy .... when he was sober. When he drank, which was often, his demeanor changed and he became an angry, raging drunk. Often to the point of violence. His intoxication often incited a fist fight at a bar. Trouble also followed him when he played his dumb bar tricks. He thought he was being funny when ordered a rookie bartender to pour a round of drinks for everyone at the bar. When it came time to settle the bar tab, Carrigan told the bartender that, "I never said I'd pay for those drinks." This trick got him thrown out of a bar on more than one occasion. Sometimes with a blackened eye.

Carrigan worked as a long haul truck driver and was away from the town for weeks at a time. When he did visit the area, he tried to keep an eye on Joe, often from a distance. He was curious to know how

Joe was doing. Mem had little tolerance for Carrigan but she allowed him to see Joe when he asked.

Mem always kept a close eye on Joe's uncle. As he grew into a young boy, he noticed Mem's uneasiness whenever his uncle visited. Joe didn't know that he wasn't really his uncle. Over time, Carrigan's visits became less frequent until he stopped coming around all together.

Later in life, reflecting on memories of his uncle, Joe sometimes wondered if there was something he wasn't told. Carrigan and he had a physical resemblance and they both had the same birth mark on their leg.

CHAPTER 3

His grandmother, Mem, became Joe's best friend. His surrogate mother. Like his mother, she had her own health issues, but they were of the physical kind, not psychological. Her condition resulted in the removal of her bladder which left her attached to a colostomy bag. Her frailness was never apparent to Joe. She was a tower of strength and kindness, and that's all that mattered to him.

Because of Mem's and his mother's conditions, and his absentee father, Joe was placed under the protection of the Massachusetts Department of Children and Families, a.k.a. DCF. DCF believes that every child is entitled to a home that is free from abuse and/or neglect. DCF became his legal guardian.

During weekdays Joe lived with foster families. On most weekends he was able to be with Mem. He loved her very much as she was, in many ways, his real mother. She was his one-and-only true companion, his rock-solid support structure. One activity that both loved was fishing. On many weekends Mem would pack a lunch, put the fishing gear in the trunk of the car, and drive them to their favorite fishing hole.

Joe did not have a grandfather, but he did have a great grandfather. From any young boy's perspective, great grandparents are very old. Their age did not alter the fact that they had a lasting influence on his work ethic and moral compass.

His great grandfather was a wise old Italian man who still spoke frequently in his native language. He provided Joe with many of the male influences that he'd not otherwise have. Albeit with a stern demeanor, he provided Joe with the lessons of hard work, dedication, commitment, and honesty.

As a rebellious youth, still younger than a teenager, Joe lived with his great grandparents for a period of time. His foster families were temporary and did not always provide a loving environment. Not surprising, given the hand that life had dealt to him, Joe often acted defiantly. He hated authority and rebelled against it. In his mind, authority figures existed only to discipline him and tell him what he was doing wrong. Adults were not his friends.

One day, when he was living with his great grandparents, he announced to his great grandfather that he was no longer going to go to school. He complained that he hated his teachers and had no use for the lessons he was expected to learn in their class-

CHAPTER 3

rooms. Great Grampa saw this as an opportunity to teach his rebellious great grandchild one of life's important lessons. He was not going to let Joe quit school. Great Grandpa had a plan, and part of that plan was to tell Joe he had a choice. In his thick Italian accent, he told Joe, "You haffa choice. You can stay in school or get a job." Joe chose that later. He was fed-up with school. He couldn't believe that a real job could be as bad, or worse.

Great Grandpa had a friend who owned a farm nearby. He dragged young Joe over to his friend's farm where he had arranged for Joe's first employment opportunity. The farmer was also an old Italian. He had rough hands from years of hard work, and sun-dried, wrinkled leather skin on his face. As the three stood there, Great Grandpa instructed his farmer friend, in Italian, "to work the Hell out of little Joe. Teach him what a hard day of work is like."

Joe was elated that he had successfully gotten out of having to go to school. And with that triumph, there was the added bonus that he'd be paid fifty cents an hour. It took only two days of farm work and Joe chose to go back to school. Work was not easier than school. In fact, it was much more difficult. Even the fifty cents per hour did not make it palatable. He learned a lesson he'd never forget. One that helped shape his life going forward.

Back in school again, Joe was cast into the life of a nomad. He'd be moved from foster home to foster home. As soon as he found comfort in one household, he'd be moved to the next. At first he resisted, and would kick and punch the social workers whose job it was to move him to his next temporary station. It was an emotional and physical struggle that he never won. To protect himself, he learned to always keep his guard up and not let himself become too comfortable lest he's be hurt and disappointed again. It was not an environment that had much potential to lead him toward anything but a life of rebellion.

There were periods of time when his mother was lucid enough to be released from the hospital. During those times, she'd attempt to provide some much needed mothering to Joe. Her efforts often ran short when her medications failed to work or she stopped taking them. The feelings he had for his mother were tempered by the fact that it was not her fault that she acted the way she did. He learned to accept his mother's disabilities, but he still craved her affection and was thankful when she was able to tender it.

All the while, he'd at least have one thing to look forward to. He'd get to spend most weekends fishing, or just being with Mem. She was the only true constant in his life, the only soul he truly loved and trusted. Without her, he may have never learned what it is like to love and trust another being.

Most of the families he lived with were well meaning and caring. They would make a sincere effort to provide Joe with a safe and loving environ-

CHAPTER 3

ment, yet there were some who only tolerated Joe to get the paycheck provided by the state. Others had a more heinous intent.

There was a time, after being in the 'system' for some time, when he was taken-in by the family of his uncle; his mother's brother. His uncle and aunt had an adopted son as well as a biological daughter. His uncle was a Viet Nam vet which may have accounted for his volatile temper.

Their daughter, Joe's cousin, did not like to share the parental attention she was used to. She plotted revenge on Joe and would often make up stories to get him in trouble. All she would have to do is simply tell her mother that Joe had stolen a toy of hers, and then watch with pleasure as Joe was punished.

Her mother's method of punishment was to hold little Joe in a head lock and pour a can of hot peppers into his mouth. If hot peppers weren't within reach, Tabasco sauce was a suitable substitute. Joe resisted the undeserved punishment, but his aunt was bigger and stronger than him. And besides, he was still a young boy and trying his best to fit in. In his mind, he wondered if he had done something wrong that merited this treatment.

One day, Joe's uncle happened to arrive home from work just as a punishment was being administered. He walked into the house and saw what was happening. He reacted with angry rage as he screamed at his wife. His volatile temper took over as he picked up a beer mug within his reach. With a mighty swing of his arm, that beer mug sailed across the room, missing the occupants, and crashed through the large picture window in the living room. The mug and broken glass sprinkled loudly onto the street outside. The house was in chaos. Joe ran from his aunt as she cowered the wrath of her husband.

Neighbors called 911 after hearing the commotion, the screaming and sound of glass shattering. A few minutes later squad cars arrived with lights and sirens blaring. After the police had the situation under control, the Department of Child Services personnel appeared at the scene and Joe was rushed off to yet another foster home.

Once again, Joe was inserted into the home of strangers. Each family had their own set of rules and expectations. Albeit most offered a loving environment, Joe learned to be cautious. Every new domicile taught him a new lesson on how to fit in, how to get along and how to survive.

Joe always looked forward to the weekend when he would be with Mem. Knowing that he'd see her on the weekends gave him the hope and strength he needed to tolerate his living conditions during the week. Just knowing that she'd show up on Saturdays gave him strength to endure. On one Saturday, Joe was sitting in the passenger seat as he and Mem drove through Leominster. While passing near the center of town, he spotted a woman sleeping on a park bench. He immediately recognized her. It

CHAPTER 3

was his mother. He yelled, "Mem, pull over, there's Mom!" Joe's grandmother refused and kept on driving. "She's doing what she wants to do Joe. Just leave her alone." They kept driving. Joe didn't understand as he bent his neck to watch his mom as long as he could. To him, Mem was always right, so he accepted her words and let it pass.

At the end of a typical weekend with Mem, she'd wash his clothes and make sure he had a good meal. Before she'd take him back to his foster home, Joe would take a shower and she'd put him in pajamas. He'd be clean and ready for bed when she delivered him home on Sunday evenings.

Joe had been living with yet another family for a few months. They treated him indifferently until one Sunday evening. Joe's grandmother, in her usual way, dropped him off at the foster home. When Joe arrived, his foster dad was the only one there. Usually, Joe would have gone straight to bed after arriving, but this night was different. The foster dad ordered Joe to take a shower before he went to bed. Joe sensed something was not right. He told his foster dad he had already taken a shower and was going to his room, but his foster dad shot back, "Go take a shower". Joe tried to reason with the man, but eventually gave in. As a young boy, this man was an intimidating figure and Joe didn't want to make trouble. He took a shower, but in the back of his mind, he felt something was not right.

The bedroom Joe was assigned to was only a short distance from the bathroom. After showering, he dried himself off, wrapped a towel around his waist and walked to his room. He expected to get dressed again in his pajamas and go to bed.

When Joe stepped through his bedroom door, he heard it slam behind him. He quickly turned around as his foster dad was locking them both inside the room. Joe's instincts had been correct, something was not right and now he knew what his foster dad had in mind. Joe had to act fast. Fearing for his safety, he wrapped his hand in the towel and smashed the window next to his bed in an attempt to escape. With a crash, glass went flying everywhere. They were on the second story of the house so Joe hesitated to jump out. Just then, the big man tried to grab him. Joe dodged his grasp and picked up a shard of glass. He plunged the sharp end into the side of the man trying to attack him. The razor sharp dagger slipped easily between the ribs of his attacker.

As the man fell to the floor in agony, Joe climbed through the open window and jumped to the ground 10 feet below. People in the neighborhood had heard the glass breaking and now they watched as a naked ten year old boy jumped to safety. The police arrived shortly thereafter and found the foster parent on the floor in the bedroom, bleeding and unable to breathe. A piece of glass was protruding from his rib cage.

Joe was moved again to another foster home.

CHAPTER 4

June 6, 1984 is a day cemented in Joe's memory. A time stamp on his soul. The events on that date that set the course in his remaining school years, and beyond. What little love and stability he had in his life was whisked away. The fragile thread that bound his sense of belonging snapped on that June day. His grandmother, Mem, died. Mem had been his mother and father wrapped into one. Now she was gone. Now Joe felt totally isolated, completely on his own.

He was only eleven years old. Mature beyond his years, but still vulnerable. Like any eleven year old boy, he had one foot behind him in childhood, and the other foot stepping forward into the abyss of adulthood. Without a loving mentor, a person he could trust and admire, the path that lay before him was precarious.

To Joe, the colostomy bag was just something that Mem wore. It never got in the way of their fishing trips, or her love for Joe. He never saw it as a warning sign, or a clue that Mem was not healthy. At eleven, Joe just didn't understand.

He asked his foster parents, "Why did she die?" Why hadn't anyone warned him that this could happen, that it was even a possibility? He didn't understand what death was and it hit him square in the face. Mem just died and never came back to see him again.

When Mem died, an angry person was born. Death had never been in Joe's vocabulary. It never occurred to him that Mem was old and fragile. Nor did it cross his young mind the absolute finality that death would bring.

Joe's anger turned outward. No one had prepared him and he was mad. Mad at the world and everyone in it. Mad at his teachers, mad at the people he thought should have warned him, and mad at himself for not understanding death.

Joe's school work began to suffer. He lashed out at everyone around him. He argued with his teachers and picked fights in school. He fought often and even began to enjoy the feeling of hitting someone and getting hit.

Already jaded by past experiences, he lost all respect for adults. To Joe, adults were the enemy. They weren't honest. They were evil and not to be trusted. He saw that his classmates were being lied to by their parents. They laughed at him when he told them he didn't believe in Santa Claus. In a strange way, he envied them in the protected cocoons their

CHAPTER 4

parents spun around them. He felt invisible to the Santa Clauses of the world. No one cared about his feelings, his needs, or his comforts.

Oddly, the death of his grandmother gave him a new sense of freedom. Feeling isolated also made him believe that he had total control of his future. There was no longer that one person to lean on and to give him direction. The only person he had loved and trusted was no longer.

The foster care system still provided food and shelter, but emotionally he was completely on his own. He no longer found it necessary to fit in, garner anyone's affections, or follow society's rules. He was navigating life on his own without a compass, but he felt in control.

One day after school, Joe happened to be searching for something to quell his boredom, so he turned on the television. The channel selector landed on a reporter interviewing President Ronald Reagan and First Lady Nancy Reagan. They were talking about the 'Just Say No' program being championed by the First Lady. In the interview, President Reagan said in so many words, "If you hang out with drug dealers and bad people, you will become one. If you want to be successful, hang out with successful people." Joe thought about those words. That simple message had a profound impact on Joe. He wanted to be successful. He had something to prove to the people who doubted him, the kids who put him down. He wanted to prove that he was worth something. The words of Ronald Reagan would, in time, be the motivation for him to make something of himself.

Even with the President's words in his mind, his anger would often boil over in school. He wouldn't follow teacher's rules. Instead he'd tell them how it was going to be. His attitude didn't sit well with most teachers. There were, however, a few who had sympathy for his situation and gave him extra space. Those few understood that his home-life was not the soft cushion afforded his other classmates.

Joe often took his anger out on his Spanish classmates. Randomly, he'd walk up to one on the school grounds and sucker-punch him in the face. There were disciplinary ramifications for his actions and revenge attacks by his nemeses. He became known around school as a fighter, a trouble maker.

No longer was Mem there to guide him, to console and love him, or teach him right from wrong. His anger boiled over spontaneously and often. He became the school bully that his biological father was before him. He was tough and would not lose a fight.

Still being 'in the system', DCF was always monitoring him. It was obvious to them that he had a high level of intelligence, but it was eclipsed by his anger. His DCF case worker sagely counseled that he needed to channel his energy and innate skills into something positive. Any activity that would occupy his time, his imagination and intelligence.

CHAPTER 4

DCF eventually gave him an ultimatum. Either he'd end his defiant behavior or be sent to a juvenile detention center. Joe chose the former. They strongly suggested that he take up a musical instrument. He chose to learn to play the drums. He didn't have money to buy a drum set, but he had a plan. One might say that it was a transformative process when Joe stole a lawnmower and sold it to pay for a set of drums. At least he was headed in the right direction.

Not long after, a music teacher introduced Joe to the saxophone. Joe had never done anything half way, and it was the same with music. He set out to learn that instrument, and become proficient enough to impress those around him. It gave him a new focus, a goal, and his concentration became a distraction to his anger. While still in the sixth grade, he studied and practiced until he played it so well that he was asked to play with the high school marching band. Music gave Joe a sense of self, a new pride, plus a new respect from his peers and teachers. It was just what DCF was hoping for.

CHAPTER 5

Being 'in the system' meant that Joe was still being moved around among numerous foster homes. In many cases, the reason he was moved was not known to him. On other occasions it was quite obvious. Otherwise, his new domicile was just another place to settle in to. Another adjustment to deal with. Stability was never a staple of his existence.

Joe spent most of his early years in Leominster, Massachusetts. He attended the Leominster schools and there he had built a network of friends. He had both good and bad experiences there, but it still was home to him.

Before he finally left foster care for good, he had lived with almost three dozen families. At one point, as a young teenager, Joe was assigned to a family in Fitchburg, MA. Leominster and Fitchburg, were neighboring towns and rival towns in the eyes of a teenager. The high schools competed against each other in sports and for bragging rights. Joe identified with Leominster. Leominster was his home town. He was a Leominster guy. All his friends lived there, but now Joe was assigned to a foster home in Fitchburg. He was not given a choice, and he felt out of place.

A small bus would pick up Joe each morning and take him from his home in Fitchburg to school in Leominster. The State felt that he should remain in the Leominster schools. The State tried to establish at least some semblance of stability in his life by keeping him in one school system. The place where his friends were, and his comfort zone.

At the end of the day, Joe would leave his friends behind and reluctantly ride the small yellow school bus back to his temporary quarters in Fitchburg. He wanted to stay in Leominster but he knew that if he wasn't on that bus each day, his absence would be reported to DCF. Joe always tried his best to stay off the DCF radar. When they showed up at the door, it often meant that he was being moved to yet another foster home. He never knew where his next destination might be.

As often as he could, after the bus dropped him off, he would walk the distance from his home in Fitchburg to hang out with his Leominster buddies. At the end of the day, he would walk back to his foster family in Fitchburg.

It was a few miles of walking in each direction, but to Joe it was worth it. One day, after walking to

CHAPTER 5

a friend's house, he was too tired to make the trek back to Fitchburg. Instead, he slept on the couch. Joe was now fifteen, and he decided that no one was ever going to tell him again where to live.

From that day on, Joe never went back to his Fitchburg family. Leominster was his home, and that is where he was determined to stay. DCF tolerated this as long as he stayed in school. No longer having a designated foster home, where he was assured a meal and a bed, he moved from friend to friend and from couch to couch. He'd live with a friend for as long as he felt welcome. As a veteran of 'the system' he knew that as long as he went to school and didn't show up on the truant list, he wouldn't trigger a response from DCF. He laid low, went to school and 'couch surfed'.

His Leominster neighborhood was a typical blue collar, middle class neighborhood with single family houses standing side by side in long rows. The streets were lined with tall maple trees and the pavement was bordered with a ribbon of cement sidewalks on both sides. Over the years, the walkway conformed to the roots that grew underneath and around the cement thus creating a pathway of contorted humps and cracks. Grass and other opportunist flora found enough free soil in the crevices to sprout new generations of greenery that conspired to widen the craters in the cement.

A neighbor, a single man about a generation older then Joe lived nearby. He made his living by operating several entrepreneurial ventures. One of his businesses was selling blankets, pottery and trinkets from a few road side stands. He'd buy Mexican goods from an importer and resell them. In his driveway was parked an old delivery truck that he was slowly converting into a mobile hot dog stand. It would eventually add to his piecemeal income. He was a friendly fellow and the neighborhood kids new him only as Victor

It was springtime. Joe had been occupying the couch at his friend Roger's house. Like most shelters in Joe's life, he accepted that this one would also be temporary. He always kept an eye out for the next sanctuary that would tolerate his nomadic existence.

The long northern winter had left maple leaves and branches scattered on the lawn after the snow had melted. The cycle of existence in the north is to prepare for the winter carnage in the Autumn, and clean up after it in the Spring. Victor's yard was in need of a Spring clean-up. The leaves and twigs begged to be raked up and discarded. That task, and some other general maintenance items around his property, would make way for the summer months ahead.

Victor offered to pay Roger for a few hours of work with a rake and a wheel barrel. He was willing to pay a reasonable wage for the labor. Joe's buddy didn't need the money and didn't really want to do the work either. Growing up in a 'normal' family, his parents would take care of his financial needs. Mon-

CHAPTER 5

ey was not something that came only as compensation for labor. He was given a weekly allowance, whether he earned it or not. He turned down the job and offered it to Joe. "You need the money more than I do. Why don't you do it?"

Couch surfing was not an easy life. Surviving by the generosity of others kept him warm in winter and put food in his stomach, but money provided more. He always had to find a way to earn his spending loot. Joe walked next door, found Victor in his back yard and said, " I hear you need someone to do some yard work. Can I have the job?"

Joe went right to work. After school, he'd walk from the bus stop directly to Victor's house. In a few days, the job was done. Victor was impressed with Joe's work. As Victor handed him the money he owed him, Joe asked, "Is there anything else you need done?" He wanted to do something else he could be paid for. Working was the only way for him to keep a few dollars in his pocket.

The neighbor was impressed with Joe's work ethic. None of the other neighborhood kids were interested in making a few dollars. In most cases, their parents gave them their spending money. Joe had only one thing with which he could barter, and that was his labor.

It might have been easier to put money in his pocket through deception or thievery, but Joe chose the honest path. The words of Ronald Reagan had become his guide, the template from which he would forge his morals. It was a decision that Joe made early in life. In spite of the hand that life had dealt him, regardless of how unfair it seemed, he was going to prove to himself and others that he could make it on his own. He'd make it with hard work, perseverance and character.

Before long, Joe had enough work to fill his time and his wallet. Among the odd jobs provided by Victor, he'd sometimes man a roadside stand selling the Mexican items that Victor bought from the importer.

He'd also work on converting the old delivery truck into that mobile hot dog stand for Victor. It eventually became street worthy and operational as a mobile kitchen. Joe now had a new job. He would park the vehicle in front of a church in Fitchburg every evening to catch the bar crowd as they came and went. The late nights impacted Joe's school work, but his priorities were elsewhere.

Eventually, Joe's couch surfing existence landed him at the residence of his employer, Victor. Joe turned a small room in Victor's house into a bedroom. This became his home for the next few years. He had successfully escaped the foster care system, and had a stable domicile. For the first time in his life, he'd occupy the same household for more than a few months at at time. Work and school kept him busy and occupied. Unwittingly, Victor became Joe's mentor. He exemplified goodness, friendship, hard work and honesty. These were the traits that pro-

CHAPTER 5

pelled Joe beyond the temptations that so many others succumb to who face similar challenges in their lives.

In high school, Joe's reputation as a fighter remained solidly intact. He'd never cower away from a threat, and people knew it. He'd win most fights, and the bullies he fought would regret they had tangled with him. Joe was a pit bull and always left his opponents damaged.

He felt that he was in charge of his life and he'd run his life as he saw fit. He announced to his teachers, "I don't do homework. I'll do my class work while I'm here, but that's it. After school I have a job. I don't have time to do homework."

His attitude did not sit well with most of the teachers. Who was he to tell them how to run their class? They all knew his living situation and his life story, but most didn't care. They had their own jobs to do. A few of his instructors accepted that his circumstances were different and they gave him a pass on doing homework. His other teachers eventually gave in, albeit reluctantly. However, they still didn't like the idea that a student was making his own rules.

For Joe, his paying job was necessary for survival. He needed to keep a few dollars in his pocket. His job kept him too busy to do homework. Something had to be sacrificed, and school work was the loser. He would have quit school altogether, but Joe knew that attending school was the best way to keep DCF out of his life. His goal was to stay off their radar screen. Otherwise, in his young mind, going to school offered him little value.

Being a good looking kid, a tough guy, and the son of the father he never knew, Joe had an eye for pretty women. His reputation at school was eerily similar to the one his father had. He fought, he was tough, the guys respected him and several girls craved his attention. It wasn't long before a pretty young gal became his steady girlfriend.

Joe would walk with her between classes and carry her books. They were a couple, and it didn't go unnoticed among his friends and foes.

Massachusetts is a state that welcomed immigrants from Puerto Rico. Many had settled in the smaller cities where they formed their own microcommunities. Leominster was one of the towns where they congregated. There were many Spanish speaking students in the high school that Joe attended.

In the school halls and outside, they'd wander in packs. From the strength of numbers, they'd taunt Joe when they saw him. Joe couldn't understand the Spanish words they hurled at him, but the message was unmistakable. They didn't like him and they expected the same in return. Whenever Joe found the opportunity, he'd pick a fight with one.

One day, Joe walked into the lunch room with a tray of food in his hands. The green tray had embossed compartments molded into it to hold food

CHAPTER 5

and keep the portions separated. In the largest compartment, Joe was carrying a big pile of steaming mashed potatoes, topped with hot gravy and chunks of white turkey meat.

As he departed the cafeteria line and looked for a seat, Joe spotted his girlfriend. She was sitting at a long table with a dozen or so students, all engaged in conversation. To her immediate left sat Rico, one of the Puerto Rican kids who liked to taunt Joe. Until now he was always insulated from Joe by the safety of a pack of his Hispanic friends. For some reason, today he decided to taunt Joe without his protective shield surrounding him. It was a risk he'd regret.

When Rico saw Joe approaching, he leaned closer to Joe's girlfriend and draped his arm around her and over her shoulder. Joe's gal leaned away and tried to free herself of Rico's arm.

Joe's response was predictable and Rico should have expected a harsh reaction. Maybe he thought he could move faster than Joe and show him who was the true tough guy. A dumb idea at best.

Joe, being only a few steps away, quickened his pace as he cocked the tray of food as if he was at home plate about to swing at a fast ball. With a round house swing, Joe planted the pile of steaming hot mashed potatoes smack in center of Rico's face. With a sound like the crack of a bat, food went everywhere as Rico fell back on the floor. Everybody in the cafeteria turned toward the sound as Joe stood over Rico.

For the next several days, Rico sported a swollen face with second degree burns, a black eye, and a bruised ego. Joe was given a few days off as punishment by the school's principal. To Joe, it was more like a vacation, or even a reward for a job well done. Hardly a comeuppance. Joe returned to class a few days later.

On his return, Joe was careful not to be in a situation where he might be outnumbered by a band of his archenemies. If they had the chance to corner him, they would show no mercy. Joe's life was truly in danger. One-on-one, no one wanted to mess with him, but a pack of angry wolves might eat him alive.

One of Joe's teachers, Mr. Melendez, owned an antique store in downtown Leominster. He was also an auxiliary police officer. Being Puerto Rican he did not like the way Joe treated his fellow countrymen. He did not like that Joe was given special treatment with his homework. And he especially didn't like the fact that Joe had humiliated his nephew with the steaming pile of mashed potatoes.

Joe's assigned seat was near the front of Mr. Melendez's classroom. Just a few steps from the chalkboard. The students all sat in hard wooden seats. There was a platter attached to the right arm of the chair. A surface for them to place books or paper to write on. Under the seat was a shelf for storing books, pocketbooks, and other accouterments.

When the homework assignments were collected, Joe, as usual, did not have his. Mr. Melendez

CHAPTER 5

took this opportunity to berate Joe in front the class. "What makes you so special tough guy?" He continued to humiliate Joe as he sat there silently getting angry. Joe's mind went into a slow, silent burn as his anger boiled over. He thought to himself, "He'll get away with it now, but when the time is right, I'll get this guy. I'll humiliate him in front of everybody like he's doing to me."

As Mr. Melendez kept up his verbal assault of Joe, he just fidgeted silently in his chair. His foot felt something on the shelf under the chair. It was a three inch thick, hardcover book. A Webster's Dictionary.

When Mr. Melendez finally ran out of insults to throw in Joe's direction, he resumed the day's lesson. Joe was still steaming and looking for an opportunity to strike back. Standing in front of the class, Mr. Melendez turned to write something on the chalkboard. Joe saw his chance, but he had to move fast.

He reached under his seat and grabbed the dictionary. It felt heavy in his hands. With a few quick steps he slipped in behind Mr. Melendez who was still writing on the chalkboard. With both hands holding the dictionary, Joe swung the book toward Mr. Melendez just as he turned his head back toward the class. With all his might, Joe hit him square in the face. Right there in front of all his classmates who had just sat through Mr. Melendez's verbal attack on Joe.

With a loud 'thwack', Melendez flew back and hit the back of his head on the chalkboard with a second resonating bang. The fight was on. Melendez grabbed Joe by the arm and launched him through the door into the hall. Joe slid head first into a row of metal lockers. He got on his feet preparing for Melendez to attack again. With rage in his eyes, Melendez charged toward Joe, but Joe was younger, smaller and faster. As hard as he could he placed a well-aimed kick between Melendez's legs. The pain brought Melendez to his knees on the hard linoleum floor.

Joe sprinted down the hall to the principal's office. Until now, the office had been a place to avoid. Nothing good ever happened there. Now it was a refuge, a safe haven. Joe knew he'd end up there anyway.

Melendez was not far behind. Running after Joe, he arrived a few seconds later. Both he and Joe were out of breath and panting. Their clothes were disheveled as if they had been in a fight. In fact they had been fighting, and it was obvious to the principal.

"Call the police", Melendez screamed. Joe yelled back, "Go ahead. Bring them on. You assaulted me." The principal stepped between the two before they could attack each other again.

Joe knew that the law did not allow a teacher to put a hand on a student. This time, the law would

CHAPTER 5

work in his favor, even though he was the one who was first to strike.

"I dare you to call them," Joe continued. There was a classroom full of witnesses that would back up Joe's claim that he was manhandled by Melendez.

The principal knew the law as well, and so did Melendez, a policeman. They also knew what a troublemaker Joe was. In the end, Joe was given a week of in-school suspension and Melendez was allowed to keep his job.

In-school suspension is an alternative setting that many schools use for disciplinary action. It removes a student from classes for a period of time while still allowing the student to attend school and complete their assignments. Joe spent the entire school day, for a week, in a designated room and was given his school work to be completed there. Most of the time, he'd be monitored by a member of the school staff who'd be in the room with him.

It didn't bother Joe that he'd be kept separate from his classmates. The room he was assigned to was occupied by a few other offenders being disciplined. He still found plenty of opportunity to raise havoc with his fellow inmates. Whenever the school staff member was not present, Joe would take the opportunity to pick a fight with an Hispanic. It was no secret that Joe hated Puerto Ricans, and the feelings were mutual. They'd use the same opportunity to pick a fight with Joe.

Between class times is when they were often left alone for several minutes. The teacher watching them had other assignments and would leave the room before the next monitor would arrive.

A few days into his in-house suspension, Joe was raising havoc with others in the room. It was during a time while supervision was absent. Joe knew that they would be alone for ten minutes or so before the next monitor would show up.

In walked Rodriguez, a member of one of the Hispanic gangs. At six foot two, he's a danger to Joe's five foot five. Joe didn't see him enter. Crouching down, Rodriguez pulled out a knife and quickly snuck up behind Joe. As he did so, he wrapped his arm around Joe putting him in a headlock. Rodriguez did not speak English, but Joe needed no translation when Rodriguez threatened to stab him.

From his days of street fighting, Joe had learned a few tricks and defenses. As Rodriguez brought the knife around in front of Joe's face, he slipped his own arm under the arm holding the knife. With all his strength he pushed on that arm before the knife could be plunged into his head. His quick move may have saved his life, but it did not save his right ear. The knife edge sliced a line through the middle of his ear and almost cut it in half. Blood started streaming down Joe's neck.

Joe twisted himself out of Rodriguez's grasp. He cocked his arm back and put his full might into a swing that caught Rodriguez square in his mouth.

CHAPTER 5

Joe punched him so hard that he thought he might have broken a bone in his hand. Rodriguez flew back onto the floor which gave Joe a split second to sprint out of the room through the open door. Some of the others in the suspension room were also gang members. It was a certainty that they would jump in the fight any second.

As Joe fled, blood flew everywhere from the wound on his hand. There was a painful gash on his middle knuckle and the skin bulged above it. Blood was oozing from the cut on his ear and his neck and shirt were now covered in blood.

Hearing the commotion and seeing Joe covered in blood, a teacher in the hall grabbed him and marched him down to the school nurse. The nurse examined him and called an ambulance. Joe was driven to the emergency room at the local hospital.

The emergency room doctor carefully stitched Joe's ear back into a single piece before he began to work on his hand. The nurse rinsed the blood from Joe, all the while she scolded him for fighting in school. It appeared that the wound on his hand would need a few stitches as well.

At first, the hump under the skin behind Joe's knuckle perplexed the doctor. He probed and poked at it. An X-ray determined that is was one of Rodriguez's front teeth. It had snapped off when Joe punched him and it was now stuck under the skin in Joe's hand. After several attempts with tweezers, the doctor was able to pull the tooth out from under the flap of skin.

While the doctor was working, the nurse continued to scold Joe. Before long, Joe had taken all he could from the nurse and stormed out of the emergency room. He left with an open wound before the doctor had a chance to stitch it closed. When Joe finally arrived at Victor's house, he used superglue to close the wound. It seemed to be an OK substitute for stitches.

CHAPTER 6

Joe's life, to this point, had been a study in bad luck. Beginning from the moment he entered into this world his very existence was challenged almost on a daily basis. There were countless times when he might have been seriously injured or killed, but he always managed to escape.

Joe sometimes wondered if he had a guardian angel. A spiritual force that shone a light on the path he should take when he strayed too far off course. Was it the words of Ronald Reagan or was it something bigger? He often thought about Mem and the lessons she had taught him, the love she had shown him, and the path she tried to pave for him.

At the end of his senior year, when high school ended, Joe's friends slowly dispersed as their lives took them toward other dreams or obligations. Some went to college, others to military service and some just drifted away. Once again, Joe felt abandoned. Being alone to chart his own path was a familiar feeling, but still unsettling.

At eighteen, no longer a ward of the state, Joe found himself with a new freedom. It was the first time in his life when no one was trying to control him. It was a freedom he had always craved, but now it seemed like a curse. He no longer had the protection that the school and state agencies provided. He once thought their umbrella was an intrusion, and now he was on his own. On his own with no one to pick him up when he fell.

He had few options. College was not affordable and military life too confining, Joe set out to find his future.

CHAPTER 7

After graduating, Joe found work at a funeral home. His job was to prepare the burial place at cemeteries, the final resting spot for the deceased before a ceremony took place. In that endeavor, one of his duties was to erect a small tent at the site next to the grave. He took pride in his role of preparing the location for the friends and family members of someone who had passed away. One of his other tasks was to make the cement cask that would be placed in the ground to accept the casket.

Joe was often alone while working in cemeteries. The rows of head stones made him reflect on the lives of the deceased that surrounded him while he worked. The loss of Mem reminded him of his own suffering. His own loss built empathy for those at each funeral site he prepared.

His surroundings made him contemplate his theories about religion. One day he asked his boss, the funeral director, how he deals with the fact that he serves all religions. The director told him to look at how the Native Americans view life and death. They see spirituality in their surroundings. Following an eagle may lead them to food. The light of the sun helps them find their way. Spirituality is not words in a book but the life around them. Factual or not, Joe began to suspect that one's spirit lives on beyond death.

Joe thought about what the funeral director told him as he worked casting a concrete vault one day for the next burial. To create a vault, he and another worker poured concrete into a large mold. By the following day the concrete had hardened. Joe would use a small crane to lift the vault onto a flatbed truck to deliver it to the burial site. At the cemetery, he would lower the vault into the hole in the ground which had already been dug by a grave digger. After the ceremony under the tent, the casket and the deceased would be lowered into the vault and sealed for all eternity.

Joe was running late one day that a vault was to be delivered. He would have to scramble to get the vault in place, set-up the tent and chairs up and clean up around the area. With no time for breakfast, he grabbed his wallet and climbed into the cab of the truck. He was behind schedule and had to hurry.

The big truck with its heavy load made it slow going on the narrow meandering roads. His pathway to the cemetery took him through several small towns.

CHAPTER 7

Where the road bent through forest and fields they were sided by ancient stone walls. These roads began their duty as foot paths and horse trails. Farmers of another lifetime had cleared their fields of stones and placed them in parallel rows. They were wide enough to navigate their horse drawn buggies, yet barely enough for two modern vehicles to pass by one another. Today the stone walls stand as a reminder of a time long ago.

Joe had just enough time to seek out a quick meal at a restaurant as he drove through one small town. To his dismay, his wallet was empty and he had no credit cards. He searched to the bottom of his pants pockets for some coins, but came up with only lint and dirt.

With work to do, and an approaching deadline, he tried to ignore the growling coming from his belly. Work that day would be a little harder with an empty stomach, but the funeral would begin soon, and his job must be completed by then. A procession of automobiles would arrive with somber mourners who were closing a chapter in their lives. It would be an embarrassment to the funeral company if the site was not ready for the internment. And it might also cost Joe his job.

It was a cold autumn day and the wind was blowing hard. The dismal sky was an appropriate backdrop for the scene unfolding. A grave digger had been to the site the previous day to excavate the hole for the burial. His skill with a backhoe, learned from many years of experience, left a nicely carved pit in the ground, with sharp corners and edges. There was barely enough room, yet just the correct dimensions to fit a concrete crypt.

Joe parked his vehicle next to the grave site. With the crane on the truck, he began to lower the cement crypt into the hole. As he was maneuvering it into place, some dirt from the top edge of the hole fell into the container. With such a snug fit, it wasn't unusual to nudge some dirt into it as he worked it into the pit.

After he carefully settled the crypt into place, Joe climbed out of the truck cab and walked to the edge of the hole. He inspected the upper edge to be certain that it was below ground level. On the floor of the crypt there was a small pile of dirt where it had spilled in. Driven by his respect of the mourners, he lowered himself into the cement box to remove the pile of dirt. He and his employer always wanted to make the scene as clean and comfortable as possible for the bereaved. The chairs had to be neatly lined up under the tent, and the surrounding landscape should be clean of any litter or debris. This included the cement box, the eternal resting place of a loved one.

While sweeping the dirt up with a small broom, Joe crouched down below the surface to avoid the cold, howling autumn wind. His ears were stinging and his stomach was still growling. To help maintain some warmth he remained crouched down in the

CHAPTER 7

crypt for a few minutes after cleaning up the dirt. Whenever he raised his head above ground level, the cold hands of the bully winds would slap him in the face. Autumn leaves and twigs would careen by his head, carried by the air currents. Just as he poked his head over the top, a leaf stuck to the side of his face. Joe reached up and peeled it off. To his surprise, it wasn't a leaf. It was a twenty dollar bill.

With the twenty in his hand and his head just above ground level, Joe made a three hundred sixty degree spin to look around for the person who might have lost the bill. There was no one in sight. Only rows of granite head stones, some of which had been there for centuries. No one had been in the cemetery since he arrived. He was alone. Except for the deceased.

What had just happened? Was it just crazy luck, or was it something more? As he looked around the cemetery he had the eerie feeling that someone was watching him. He was hungry and cold, and until that moment, had no money. Was Mem watching over him? Joe pondered these questions as he stuffed the bill in his pocket.

Later in the day after the ceremony had ended, Joe was folding up the tent and stacking the chairs, and preparing to drive back to the funeral home. The grave digger arrived with his equipment to cover the grave site with soil and sod. Joe asked him, "Do you carry cash?" He answered, "Why do you ask?" Joe asked again a little more forcibly, "Just answer the question. Do you carry cash?" The grave digger, slightly annoyed at Joe's demeanor replied, "No. Why?" Thinking that *this is just too weird,* he told the grave digger "I found 20 bucks and you're the only other person who was here before me."

Joe's mind reeled with both wonder and amusement as he absorbed what just happened. *Did the dead person I am serving today send his appreciation from the other side? Or was it Mem?*

CHAPTER 8

One of his old high school buddies, Mitch Sullivan, had move to Florida before their senior year. Mitch's father had retired and chosen the southern state to make a new home. Mitch missed his Massachusetts friends and had kept in touch with Joe. Mitch had always admired Joe and envied his freedom. The freedom to make his own decisions and not to be told what to do every day by overbearing parents. What he didn't understand was that Joe's life only appeared to be easy. The underlying reality contradicted the facade.

A year or two after Joe had finished high school, Mitch coaxed him to come south and stay with him and his family. Florida seemed so far away. It was a place he had often heard about. Joe had sometimes let his imagination wander over the pictures he had seen of sandy white beaches that stretched into the horizon. It was a post-card location. The beaches were bracketed by a row of palm trees and a turquoise ocean. The job at the funeral business had put money in his pocket, but he wanted more. Florida always looked like a place he might like to visit. And besides, it would be a nice place to escape the memories of his surroundings. Florida might be a good place to start over.

Joe bought a bus ticket to North Port, Florida. He hoped that what lay ahead of him was a new beginning, a manifestation of his unchecked freedom. To Joe it was the dawn of an adventure and a new start in his life. He wasn't sure where his life was headed, but he wanted to find out. Excitement welled in his being, yet apprehension controlled his enthusiasm. He had had too many failed hopes in his life to be blinded by another Utopian desire. He dreamed about the possibilities on the bus ride south.

A few days later he arrived in Florida. Mitch and his father met him at the bus terminal. While Mitch greeted Joe with a smile, obviously happy to see his friend, Joe did not sense a similar warmth from Mitch's father. Over his short lifetime, Joe had developed a six sense, more generally described as 'street smarts' when it came to sizing up people or measuring his surroundings. Mr. Sullivan's demeanor made him feel uncomfortable. Joe's street smarts engaged and initiated a subliminal measure of caution.

Mr. Sullivan was a retired Massachusetts police officer. He had moved his family to Florida to retire

CHAPTER 8

but, more so, he used the distance to escape the past. There were too many miscreants in his old surroundings for him to feel safe in his retired years. He feared that there were many whom he had arrested who might seek retribution. That perceived threat, though maybe far-fetched, bolstered his paranoia enough to cause him to uproot his family and move them to another state. A state with many miles between it and Massachusetts.

Having spent many years in 'the system' and having to readjust to yet another home, this was nothing new. Be polite, follow the rules and do what you are told. It was what he did, how he survived and how his life had unfolded.

Joe moved in with his 'new family'. Until Joe arrived, his new family was a family of five. With a bother and a sister, Joe's buddy, Mitch, was the youngest child. The older siblings Jimmy, and Christina accepted Joe into the family.

Mitch was still in awe of Joe. There was something about his carefree, self-directing lifestyle that Mitch admired. He wanted to be like Joe.

It wasn't long before he sensed that he had made a mistake. One indication was that the rules he had to abide by to be accepted by his new Florida family were trivial and demeaning. The restrictions imposed on him by his host were not much different than those he had encountered while living with other families. But now, he felt that he was no longer a child in need.

Before long, the retired cop began to micro-manage Joe in irritating and baseless ways. Joe was accused of running up the electric bill. When Mr. Sullivan told him he was forbidden to eat chicken with the skin on it, Joe knew it was time to leave. He didn't have to put up with this any longer. He was old enough to make his own way without being micro-managed by a father he didn't love and who didn't love him.

The confidence that comes with age strengthened his notion that a meal and a bed were no longer worth the price of abiding by the petty rules being imposed on him by the father of his friend. He was now old enough, smart enough and ambitious enough to provide for himself.

Even though he had been in the area for only a short time, Joe had already made a few friends. Like him, they were street-smart and knew their way around. One of them had had a similar upbringing as Joe and had also learned to survive on his own. He too had ventured out and even had his own apartment. Eager to get out from under the control of the retired cop, Joe move into the apartment with his friend and took up a spot on the couch.

In only a matter of days he landed a job at the Tampa Tribune selling newspapers. It was the perfect job for him. His income was based on how much he was willing to work. Joe was in control of his destiny again. He was no stranger to hard work and he made good money. Sales came naturally to

CHAPTER 8

him. His life had been a study in meeting and befriending all sorts of people, and finding ways to convince them to do something for him. In the past it might have been getting an extra helping on his plate, now it was exchanging a newspaper for their money. He was good at it.

When Joe earned enough money he decided to go back home. Florida had not been all that he expected it to be. He had not found what he was looking for. Now his old life beckoned him back to New England. He yearned for the familiar backdrop of his old neighborhood. It was familiar territory and still felt like home. Joe bought a bus ticket to take him back to Fitchburg, Massachusetts

He wasn't angry at anyone or anything - quite the opposite. He was thankful of the life he had had. Be it the message from Ronald Reagan, or some innate moral guide, he was determined to do good, to make a difference. It was always his nature to be upbeat.

The challenges of growing up in 'the system' provided an education that is not given in a class room. He had acquired both book-smarts and street-smarts. Survival skills that aren't in the lesson plan of any school teacher. His classroom was 'the system', the foster homes, DCF, and the street.

The Greyhound Bus dropped him off in his old surroundings. With money in his pocket, renting an apartment was within his reach. A job came next.

It took more than one job to pay the rent and to put food in his belly. Between a job driving a limousine and another detailing cars for a local dealership, he was paying the bills. Yet with the creature comforts taken care of, he needed a little extra to entertain a young lady. She was a pretty gal he had dated back in high school. Before long they started seeing each other again.

He started playing in a band on his days off. His skills as a drummer were known to those in the small circle of amateur musicians in the area. It was a fun distraction from the boredom of his jobs, and he always wondered if it could blossom into something bigger. Making music was fun and money from making music was even better.

At the car dealership, Joe's job was to recondition the used cars on the lot, keep the new cars clean, and to detail customer's cars. One day he heard a customer yelling angrily at one of the car salesman. He heard something said about scratches on the side of a car that weren't there when the customer dropped his car off for maintenance.

Joe watched and listened for a few minutes before he interjected himself into the conversation. He introduced himself, and his boss watched as he calmed the customer down. He explained that the scratches may have been made by neighborhood kids. Sometimes, after dark, the kids would cut through the parking lot. The car may have been scratched by one such trespasser after hours. Joe then went to work and buffed out the scratches. The customer left happy, and thanked Joe for what he had done.

CHAPTER 8

The manager, having witnessed it all, thanked Joe for how he handled the situation. The results could have been an angry customer leaving the property, probably never to return. Instead, Joe had taken control of the situation, quelled the customer's anger and provided a solution. The person left satisfied, and will probably remain a customer. Joe saved the day.

This one simple act was the beginning of a lucrative career in the car business. His life was also changing in a another way. He had proposed to and married his girlfriend. Life was taking on a new dimension for Joe. He was happy and his future looked promising.

Fitchburg, is situated in north, central Massachusetts on the shores of the Nashua River. Today, it is the third largest city in Worcester County, with a population slightly greater than 40,000. In the 19th-century it was an industrial center. Like many American cities, both large and small, it had its origin on a river that provided water power for manufacturing industries. The fast flowing river water was harnessed to spin water wheels thus providing inexpensive power. That power was transferred by mechanical means to factories situated along the banks of the river. The water would drive shafts, pulleys, and belts that ran milling machines. The large mills produced machine parts, tools, clothing, paper and firearms. In its heyday, Fitchburg was an economic power house.

The city prospered from a second economic engine as well. The Fitchburg Railroad ran through Fitchburg and the Hoosac Tunnel, linking Boston to Albany, New York. The tunnel was built using the Burleigh Rock Drill, which was designed and built in Fitchburg.

Built from 1851-1875, the Hoosac Tunnel is a 4.75-mile railroad tunnel in western Massachusetts that passes through the Hoosac Range, an extension of Vermont's Green Mountains. "Hoosac" is an Algonquian Indian word meaning "place of stones". At the time of its completion, the tunnel was the world's second-longest, after the 8.5-mile Mont Cenis Tunnel through the French Alps. The Hoosac tunnel is still in operation today.

As time passed, water power was obsoleted by more versatile and reliable forms of energy and the old mills fell into disrepair. Mostly abandoned, they sat deteriorating for decades along the Nashua River. In the late 1990's there was one such mill in Fitchburg that had been re-purposed. It was a two story brick building. The first floor had been refurbished, but the second story remained in unusable condition.

The street level had been converted into rooms that were rented to aspiring musicians. It provided a space where they could meet and rehearse. Almost 25 different bands rented space to practice. The building was far enough away from any residential area to be a nuisance, and the old loading docks

CHAPTER 8

made it easy for bands to move their equipment in and out. It was a friendly place to practice their art and a convenient spot to store their equipment in-between paying gigs.

One entrepreneurial musician turned a space he rented into a mini night club. His room became a popular hangout for fellow musicians. He decorated it with colored lights and curtains on the windows. There were tables and chairs and against one wall was a refrigerator that was always stocked with beer. There were amplifiers, microphones, and a public address system. He offered everything a band would need to play.

The atmosphere, and the seemingly endless supply of beer, made it a fun place to hang out and make music. The tenant himself had often tried to start his own band, but he had chronic bad luck attempting to assemble a group of musicians with the combined skills needed to produce the songs he wanted to perform. On any given weekend, many aspiring musicians would hang out there. He had an inviting room, and the beer flowed like water.

One evening Joe was there to audition for a band looking for a drummer. When he arrived, he got a phone call and was informed that the audition had been canceled. Not having much else to do, Joe took a seat and grabbed a beer from the refrigerator.

A few minutes later, in walked a character Joe had never seen before. His head was shaved bald, except for one round spot, centered just above his forehead, about an inch in diameter. From that spot grew a foot of hair. The hair was loosely braided in a ponytail and flopped around as he walked. He looked like a human unicorn. His head movement would swing the tail around in a circle. He introduced himself as Sargent Howard. Joe dubbed him the Unicorn Man.

In one hand he held an electric guitar by its neck. Most musician's cherish their instrument and protected it in a guitar case. Not the Unicorn Man. As Joe watched this character, he sauntered up to the stage and tossed his guitar up onto the hardwood surface as if it was a bag of trash. With that, he let out a roaring laugh. With beer in hand, Joe just watched in amazement as Unicorn Man climbed up on stage. This guy was really amusing.

A few minutes later, a friend of Unicorn Man walked in and jumped up on the stage. They plugged their guitars into the amplifiers and started to jam together. Thinking that their sound could use a drum beat, Joe climbed up, sat at the drums and joined in. Without much effort, and having never played together until then, they sounded pretty good.

Joe was pleasantly surprised that they all proved to be good musicians. In a few minutes, they found themselves in a nice musical groove, making some tight impromptu music. Looking at Unicorn's beat-up guitar, Joe wondered how it could sound as good as it did.

CHAPTER 8

As he played, Unicorn Man would rock his body to the beat and make that pony tail spin above his head like a helicopter blade. Joe watched in amazement, saying to himself, "Is the guy for real? If he spins that helicopter blade any faster, he'll lift off." To Joe he looked like a wild creature, but he could make good music. And as beat-up as it was, he sure knew how to make that guitar sing.

After a while, and doing what beers do, they took a break and Joe found the men's room. While answering nature's call, Unicorn Man asked Joe if he'd be willing to jam with a band he was forming. Joe had already made up his mind that they had something here, so he readily accepted the offer. After all, he had come to the old mill building that evening hoping to become a drummer in a band

As they left the men's room and walked back toward the stage, Unicorn Man yelled, "Hey Billy, get me a beer." When Billy answered, Joe thought that he had heard that voice from from somewhere before. At first he didn't recognize his face, but he slowly put it together. After listening to Billy for a minute, Joe asked, "Hey Billy, do you know who I am? Dude, you and I are cousins." Joe's mother had several siblings, and Billy was a cousin he hadn't seen since they were kids. Now they were playing on stage together.

Once again, Joe thought about Mem. *Was she manipulating Joe's life somehow from the other side? These co-*

incidences are just too strange. She even found a band for me.

One collateral effect of Joe's life in 'the system' is that he had lost contact with some of his extended family. Aunts, uncles and cousins he may have met at one time were lost to him. He didn't even know how many he had. He sometimes wondered: *Who are they? Where are they? How are they doing? What are their lives like? Do they know that I exist?* Maybe some live on the next block or even next door.

There was a guitarist that Unicorn wanted to help fill the sound the band was trying to create. He lived a few miles north in New Hampshire. Joe's cousin had his own band and was at the mill building that day just to jam with Unicorn.

Unicorn wanted Joe to meet the other guitar player. He thought that the three of them might make a good band. A few weeks later, after a short drive, Joe met the other guitar player who lived up in The Granite State. Joe and the guitarist hit it off immediately. At that meeting, the band 'SoulMine' was born. Joe on the drums, Jerry played lead guitar and Unicorn Man played bass guitar.

That day in New Hampshire, they jammed all afternoon. Their individual styles were compatible and their talents meshed well. It didn't take long for them to find a groove and produce a great sound. All the basics were there. That afternoon they knew they had the beginning of something special.

CHAPTER 8

Later in the evening, after hours of jamming, they all sat around a table to discuss what they wanted to get out of a band. They each had separate lives, needs, desires and complications to consider.

Jerry, the lead guitar player from New Hampshire was an architect and had a full time job practicing his trade. It was a good job with good pay. All he wanted from the band was a fun time jamming on weekends. To him the band was not much more than a hobby, his recreation and a way to relax after a week at the office.

Joe and Unicorn also had jobs and families. They all agreed that the playing music was just for enjoyment. Yet if the sound was right, they would make a recording and let it take on a life of its own. They had no expectations other than to have fun.

Before Joe had come into the picture, Unicorn Man and Jerry had been in a band called Bone Orchard. Bone Orchard had a good sound and was popular in the local area. They played at small venues and had a loyal following. At one time they had entered a battle-of-the-bands contest and surprised themselves by winning a prize. The prize was a recording session at a professional studio. Unfortunately for them, the Bone Orchard band broke up before they could use the recording session prize. However, the guys still had that prize in their pocket for future use. SoulMine was now in possession of that prize and it would come in handy.

Their desires and expectations were simple. Making good music was the goal they all shared. If anything else became of it, they'd deal with it as it happened. They just wanted to be creative and enjoy themselves. All in their early thirties, all employed in other jobs with their own lives, the band was mostly a hobby. Nothing serious, just good fun and good music.

After many weekends of jamming, Soul Mine had put together a short repertoire of songs. They decided to cash in their prize of the free recording session to make a demo recording. They could play the recording to prospective employers as a first step to get weekend gigs at local bars and night clubs in the area.

Each member of the band had a few copies of the demo CD to play to potential employers. One of Unicorn Man's nephews attended a small school in southern New Hampshire. He 'borrowed' one of his uncle's CDs and brought it to school to play for his friends. Unbeknownst to the band, SoulMine became a very big hit within the walls of the high school. The kids loved their sound. The high schoolers made more copies of the CD and gave them to anyone who wanted one. The school was abuzz with SoulMine music.

To help them market their name, the band had some promotional literature printed. Small leaflets, posters and stickers were handed out freely. The stickers started showing up all over the high school.

CHAPTER 8

The walls and lockers in the halls became plastered with SoulMine stickers. Once stuck to the metal surfaces, they weren't easy to remove.

One day, Joe received a message through social media from the high school principal. The principal was in the habit of monitoring web media to see what his students were up to, and it was the only way he knew how to contact members of the band. In his message he complained to Joe that SoulMine stickers had been placed all over high school property. He even went so far as to threaten to take legal action against the band for property damage.

Joe knew that the principal's threats were baseless, and instead he saw this as an opportunity where everyone could benefit. He had become adept at turning a negative situation into something positive.

Even though it wasn't the band who defaced school property, Joe attempted to remedy the situation. He decided to meet face-to-face with the principal to explore ways to stop the kids from defacing school property. At his meeting with the principal he offered to come to the school and speak to the student body at an assembly or in classrooms.

Joe reflected on his past and the chaos he had created while he was a school kid. Now, as an adult and a parent, he had empathy for the school administrators he had once tormented. He also had a keen understanding of the peer pressure and the frustrations that students deal with on a daily basis.

The principal was surprised and impressed with Joe's willingness to help, his keen understanding of adolescents and of his problem solving skills. Before the conversation ended, the principal asked if Soul-Mine would be willing to play at the school's talent show. "The kids like you." He explained. "You sound like you could be a positive role model."

That statement told Joe that the principal had not listened to their CD. It was full of profanity. Joe worried that it would send the wrong signals. Even so, the song's underlying message was about growing up in a challenging environment. Child abuse, and overcoming struggles, but all leading to a positive outcome. A synopsis of Joe's own life.

After explaining his concerns about the colorful language to the principal, Joe offered to change the words for the talent show. They shook hands, SoulMine had a new gig, and the principal had a role model for his students.

A few days later, Joe and the band drove to the school to inspect the physical layout of where they would be playing. How big was the stage? What was the best way to deliver, set-up and take-down their instruments and amplifiers? They were there only to work out the logistics of moving their equipment.

Someone must have leaked the word that they were coming, because there was a large welcoming committee in the parking lot. When their van pulled up to the school, they were mobbed by their high school fans. Many were wearing SoulMine t-shirts,

CHAPTER 8

holding posters and screaming. The kids formed a crowd around then and asked them to sign their shirts, posters and CDs. It was near chaos. SoulMine mania had engulfed the high school. The students couldn't get enough of their music. It was the first time in his life that Joe had been asked for an autograph. Not something he had expected.

After a life beginning in foster homes, and sometimes having to fight for his very survival, Joe was now a rock star. At least he was in the eyes of a local high school students. He had never doubted his own self-worth, and now it was confirmed by a crowd of admiring fans.

The bubble burst a few days later. To everyone's dismay, the principal canceled the show before the scheduled performance. The kids enthusiasm had become so intense and unruly, the principal decided to take disciplinary action against them. The band members were disappointed, but understood why the principal did what he did.

By now the band had become a local sensation. Demonstrated by the out-of-control fans at the high school. SoulMine began to book more and more shows at local taverns and music venues. Over time their music continued to improve which made the band even more popular. People in the music industry started to take notice.

SoulMine became a regular attraction at Sharkey's, a music venue in Southern New Hampshire. They developed a loyal following of fans, and would fill Sharkey's almost every night they played. Of course, the manager of Sharkey's liked the business that SoulMine brought to them.

One night, after a show at Sharkey's, a gentleman approached the band as they were taking their equipment out. He introduced himself as the program manager of a local radio station. It was a rock station whose target audience was the same fans who followed SoulMine.

The program manager told the band, "For months, we've been getting requests to play your music on the radio. We didn't even know who you are. Now I can put a face to the name" He continued, "Can we feature your music on one of our Sunday night shows called *Home Grown?*" *Home Grown* was a promotional radio program that would play exclusively the music from local bands. The band members liked the idea and readily agreed. Who wouldn't?

Soul Mine became a big hit on *Home Grown*. Their popularity was bolstered by the radio station and their talent as musicians. The radio waves increased the size of their audience and they started to get invitations to play at larger and more exclusive venues. The station assisted them in booking gigs, and in return the band would give the station their latest songs to play. It was a symbiosis they all liked.

One evening, Joe got a short-notice request from the radio station to fill a spot on the air. Another band had canceled and the station needed a favor.

CHAPTER 8

The person on the phone explained the situation. Joe accepted the job without hesitation, even before he had spoken to the other band members. He recognized it as a good opportunity, and he knew he could convince the others if they needed convincing. "We'll take the Job."

The ease in which they dealt with the radio station and venue managers helped them book bigger and better shows. Their music was good, they attracted large crowds and the business managers liked to work with them. It became a formula for success. The radio station began to call them whenever they had an opening.

One night at Sharkey's, SoulMine was billed as the opener for another band named Wednesday Widows. Wednesday Widows won the marquee spot that night because one of their members was a well-known musician, a headliner from a national act.

SoulMine arrived early to unload their equipment and set up for the show. Wednesday Widows arrived at about the same time. Unicorn Man introduced himself to the headliner. By his arrogant response, the band knew to steer clear of this guy. He made it obvious that his popularity had gone to his head and he was too self-important to pay attention, or even be courteous to members of SoulMine. The message was clear. This guy is a jerk.

Soul mine continued to set up their equipment. They would be the first band on stage, so they had to be ready. The sound manager at Sharkey's had worked with SoulMine many times over the months, so he already had them dialed into the sound console. He monitors and adjusts the sound levels before and during each performance. From the console, the sound manager can blend together the right volume and pitch levels for each instrument and microphone. In no time, Soul Mine was practicing their music. As usual it sounded great.

While they were warming up, Joe watched the members of the other band milling around. They'd huddle and talk among themselves and then mill around some more. They were not smiling.

A few minutes later, Joe spotted the club manager and Wednesday Widows' band manager in a heated discussion. He couldn't hear what was being said, but it was clearly an argument. Their body language was unmistakable. Their arms were flailing and their heads were bobbing up and down as they stood nose-to-nose yelling at each other.

A while later, after things calmed down, Joe asked the band manager what the disagreement was about. He explained, "It was about you guys." Wednesday Widows is mad at the club for booking a three-piece local band to play before their nationally known three-piece band. Wednesday Widows did not say it in so many words, but the underlying message was that they were afraid they'd be upstaged by Soul-Mine.

The show went on that night and SoulMine clearly out-played Wednesday Widows. The reaction by

CHAPTER 8

the crowd was proof enough. The claps and cheers for SoulMine overpowered the week accolades for Wednesday Widows. As it turned out, SoulMine's sound was far superior. Their singer overpowered the performance of Wednesday Widows' singer, and their music sounded tighter and well rehearsed.

After the show, Wednesday Widows packed up and left in a huff. The members of SoulMine stayed around and hung out at the back of the venue at a small table selling and signing CDs and posters to their fans. In the crowd was a guy mingling around and carrying a large sack of CDs. He was giving them out to anyone who wanted one. The CD was music by Alien Animal Farm, a band who had copied a Michael Jackson hit, but in a heavy metal style.

Out of the corner of his eye, Joe watched the guy with the CDs as he made his way to their table. Joe expected to be handed a CD. Instead the man introduced himself to the band as a street-team member of an independent record label. A street-team member is a person who reports back to the mother ship about any talented bands they had found in their territory. He asked Joe if he could buy a CD to send back to headquarters. Joe readily handed him one for free.

After the show, the three band members wondered if they'd ever hear back from the street-team member. A few weeks passed, and after another SoulMine performance, another representative from the same record company approached them. This guy was in a suit and tie and introduced himself as an agent of the company. He said, "Boys, a member of my street-team sent me your CD. I like what I heard. I'd like to talk to you about working with us." At that point he held out a packet of papers in front of them. Joe was the first to reach and take the packet from the agent.

Unicorn Man and Joe looked at each other and grinned in amazement. Could this be real? Were they being offered a recording contract? The band's singer had a different reaction. He snatched the packet from Joe's hands, reached forward and waived it in under the reps nose as he demanded, "Is this a record contract?" He received the reply, "Yes it is, we'll go over the details in a few minutes." To everyone's surprise, Jerry spit on the papers, tore them in half and dropped them on the table. Joe and Unicorn man watched the expression on the record reps face as their singer stormed out of the room. Joe and Unicorn Man were as surprised as the man in the suit.

They all wondered what had sparked that emotional outburst. Was Jerry afraid they'd lose control over the band? Was he concerned that their freedom to create their own sound might be commandeered by an outside force? Was he worried that making money for the record company would become their new mission? The only person who knew for sure was Jerry.

CHAPTER 8

After the astonishment subsided and clearer heads returned, the record company executive regained his focus on the mission to obtain a signed contract. Joe and Unicorn Man didn't need much convincing, but the other third of SoulMine had just stormed out the door. He would be difficult to convince and even more difficult to replace.

Joe and Unicorn Man wanted to learn more. Not only did they want to understand why Jerry reacted as he had, they wanted to know if this was a viable contract? And if so, was it a fair contract? They wanted to know before they made efforts to reel in Jerry. If it was a bad contract, none of them should agree to it and nothing would change.

Joe and Unicorn Man left the meeting with an unsigned contract in their possession. They told the record company agent that they'd get back to him in a few days. In the meantime, they'd find out from Jerry why he stormed out of the meeting. Maybe they could convince him to keep an open mind.

Later in the week, Unicorn Man and Joe met with Jerry to discuss the events of the evening with the record agent. He had calmed down and apologized about his emotional response. He even offered, "Let's take a closer look, maybe it's a positive step for the band."

Joe searched around and located a lawyer in Boston who specialized in the entertainment industry. For one hundred fifty dollars, the lawyer would review the contract verbiage and give his opinion.

Joe paid the one fifty and he and Unicorn Man made an appointment with the lawyer in Boston.

After looking over the document, the lawyer reported that, "This contract is one of the better contracts I have seen. There are only a few items that I recommend changing. Otherwise, it's a good contract." He continued, "If you decide to sign this contract and agree that I be your counsel, I'll refund your one hundred fifty dollars. I'd sign this contract if I were you." They left the attorney's office energized by his positive assessment. Yet they wanted to include Jerry in the decision to sign or not, so they departed with no signatures on the document.

About a week had gone by since the lawyer's blessing of the contract. That week gave Jerry time to mull over all that signing a record contract might mean. For him, becoming a full time rock star would be a major change in the direction of his life. He had a good job. He had a career from which he had pursued a lengthy and expensive education. He had to ask himself *is my career something I'd be willing to give up, or put on hold?* These thoughts had been reeling through his head for a week.

In the beginning of SoulMine, they were a garage band that played on weekends. Making music was just for fun. It was a seamless process to take it one step further by accepting some paid gigs. It was still fun, and by earning some money made it that much more enjoyable.

CHAPTER 8

Now a bigger opportunity was knocking at their door. Were they ready? Was he ready? Was he willing to risk everything for a chance at stardom? These were concerns that bedeviled him.

Joe and Unicorn Man were free to pursue that dream. Their commitment to their day jobs was not as deep as Jerry's. They could easily break free to chase stardom.

Over a beer, the three of them met to consider their options. With a recording contract their music might be played on radio stations across the country. As a band, it was the next logical step toward getting the name SoulMine on the record charts. The path to stardom lay ahead of them.

Jerry laid out his concerns to the other two. He put it like this, "If we sign a record deal, we'll probably last about five years. Not many bands make it beyond that. I'll have to give up my job as an architect and put my career on hold. After five years, my licenses will have expired and I'll have to renew them. The software tools I use will have been updated, so I'll have to retrain on how to use them. It won't be easy to restart my career. There are no guarantees that we will be a successful rock band. It's a big risk for me. I really want to make music, but I'm not sure if it's the right thing for me at this point in my life."

Later in the day, in a conversation with the record company agent, Joe described the concerns and reservations that Jerry had about signing the contract. They both felt that his concerns were understandable, but not insurmountable. The record company offered to amend the contract in an attempt to mitigate Jerry's misgivings. To minimize the travel requirements they offered to start out by promoting the band regionally as opposed to nationally. They'd only have to travel as far away as New York City. They'd start slow and could get a feel for what might lie ahead. If the band was successful and if Jerry changed his mind, they would revisit the possibility of going national.

With these changes, Jerry could keep his job as an architect. All three members of SoulMine signed the agreement. They had a recording contract. With beginnings at the dusty old warehouse in Fitchburg, the door of opportunity was now wide open.

The work began and their shows got bigger and bigger. Sometimes they were booked as the opening act for well known, national acts. On one occasion they opened for an internationally know rock band. The venue was the Worcester Centrum in Worcester, Massachusetts.

The Centrum is an indoor arena and convention center complex located in downtown Worcester, Massachusetts. It is an enormous structure with a capacity of almost fifteen thousand. It first opened in the early 1980s. The opening event was a Frank Sinatra concert. Since then, it has hosted music artists of national and international status.

SoulMine opened the show that night. Even though the seats were only a third full, the band

CHAPTER 8

members were in awe. They had made it to the big time. They were rock stars. While playing the drums, Joe looked around and reflected on where he had been. His life started out with the toughest of circumstances. From foster homes and a victim of gang violence, to a self-made businessman and now a rock star. He had beat the odds. They had arrived. He had arrived.

A few weeks later, they learned that their employer, the record company, had been sold. A larger company had bought them. This could be a good change, or the opposite. The company called and asked the band to come to New York to meet their new employer. The topic of discussion would be the terms of their contract. They didn't take this is as good sign.

Jerry was concerned. He had been juggling two lives. His day time job was demanding enough, and keeping up with SoulMine's schedule was not easy unto itself. A new contract might tip the scale for him. As far as he was concerned any changes would likely be bad changes. Jerry informed Joe and Unicorn Man, "I have a bad feeling about this." He kept his thoughts to himself that this might be the end of his time with the band.

They all met in their new employer's office in New York City. The hammer was about to fall. On the desk was a copy of their contract. The new company had decided that any contract less than eighteen months old would be terminated. Theirs was on that list. Two of the band members were heart broken, but Jerry was relieved. By terminating the contract Jerry's dilemma had just vanished. The decision had been made for him.

In the record company's office, the discussion turned to money. A check for money owed was given to the band. It was not what they had expected. A check had been cut for five cents on the dollar for every dollar of revenue they had produced for the record company.

The company had given the band cash advancements to cover their expenses. They 'graciously' offered to forgive those advances and relinquish their rights to all SoulMine songs. They tried to make it sound like they were doing the band a favor.

The band still had one more obligation to fulfill. They were booked as opening act for a nationally known band. The venue was in central Massachusetts. SoulMine played, albeit somewhat distraught. Even so, they gave a great performance. After the show they packed up their equipment and went their separate ways. SoulMine dissolved that day.

Joe's rock star ambitions were staunched by the breakup of the band. For Joe, it had been just another truncated adventure. His life to this point had been a bumpy ride, and this was just one more bump in that road. His vision of a life playing music made for wonderful daydreaming, but the reality was that it wasn't going to happen. Maybe there was a silver lining to the fact that making music had never pro-

CHAPTER 8

duced enough money to break away from his main source of income, selling cars.

Joe resigned himself to the reality that another chapter in his life had closed. His focus now shifted back to his job as a car salesman. He now had one child and bigger responsibilities as a father. Sure, he was disappointed in losing the band, but he didn't let it get him down.

CHAPTER 9

Joe's wife, Carla, came from a large family. Many aunts, uncles, cousins and siblings. The problems began when Carla's family started hanging around their house. At first, a few would stop by with a six pack and watch TV with Joe and Carla. It soon became regular habit. Before long they were attacking the refrigerator and helping themselves to whatever they found. Over time, more and more relatives would show up, unannounced, and uninvited, hungry and thirsty. They'd take over Joe's home and always leave behind a mess of beer cans and food wrappers. It bothered Joe that his generosity was being taken advantage of. None of them even offered to pay for the food they took.

Joe asked Carla to say something to her relatives, but she refused. She'd argue back, "They are my family and I have a right to share my home with them." It became a serious point of contention between Joe and Carla that drove a wedge between them. Some mornings, Joe would find people sleeping on couches and furniture. There were times when more than 20 people were hanging around in his house. When Joe was at work, they would complain to Carla about Joe's inhospitality while they were eating his food.

Joe could see that his life was once again on a downward trajectory. He was losing control of his house, his family and his temper. The arguments with Carla became more frequent and contentious. In one angry verbal exchange, she thrust a dagger into Joe's heart when she screamed that she had had an affair, and that their child was not his. He could see where this was going.

As his life began to unravel, Joe reflected on his own past as a foster child. In spite of his wife's infidelity he decided to stay with her and raise the child. He didn't want the baby to grow up without a father. He knew too well how difficult a life that is. It takes a special person to swallow their pride and put the welfare of a child before it.

Over time his unwanted guests began to show up less frequently. By keeping the refrigerator empty of beer, Joe manged to move the leaches onto other hosts. The arguments with his wife subsided and their life regained the happiness of times past.

Before long, Joe and Carla had a second child. With a growing family, the bills came faster than they could be paid. Car sales were good in some months and not so good in others. The new baby ex-

CHAPTER 9

acerbated their financial pressures. Now there were four mouths to feed, doctor bills and more clothes to buy.

Fortunately, their house had an attached in-law apartment. Renting that space helped with the bills. The income it produced filled the gaps when car sales slowed and relieved the strain on the family budget.

Joe's mother-in-law, Maud, lived nearby. She was a short, obese women who made a living selling building materials to the local tradesmen. Joe did not get along with her. Whenever she found the opportunity she would harass Joe and berate him in front of his kids and wife. She seemed to take joy in destabilizing Joe's marriage.

After days of complaining that she was not feeling well Maud announced that she had been diagnosed with liver cancer and that she was dying. It just so happened that a tenant had recently vacated the in-law apartment. She begged her daughter to let her move into the apartment so that she could be with her grandchildren until she died. After a big fight with Carla, an argument that Joe knew he would lose, he agreed to allow her mother to move in. How could he be so cruel as to not let his wife's sick mother, the grandmother of his children, not stay there until she died? There was no way he was going to win that argument.

Maud took up residence in the apartment. This put more strains on Joe's marriage. When Joe was at work, she tried to convince her daughter that Joe was having an affair. Tensions continued to rise and arguments became more frequent and vicious. Even while living on Joe's paycheck, she continued to sow the seeds of distrust between him and Carla.

Miraculously, after a few months the liver cancer disappeared. Somehow, she was cured. Not surprising in Joe's eyes. Maud plied her trade as a diabolical leach. She was a parasite that would suck the life out of her host until it died or went away.

She found a way to collect disability payments from the government by claiming she was agoraphobic. Agoraphobia is a mental disorder characterized by symptoms of anxiety in situations where the person perceives the environment to be unsafe with no easy way to escape. Joe suspected, with good reason, that she was faking it to get a paycheck from the government.

Her goal in life was to never work again and to live off the hard work of others. She paid no rent while living in Joe's house, in spite of the fact that she had an income. This did not sit well with Joe. Trying to avoid a confrontation with his wife he tried his best to keep his thoughts to himself, but sometimes his anger boiled over. He'd argue with Carla and demand to know, "Why can't your mother at least help pay for the food we feed her?"

It rubbed more salt in the wound when Maud found the time and energy to become an ordained preacher. She would often spend her time at the lo-

CHAPTER 9

cal prison, counseling and preaching to the inmates. Joe asked Carla, " If Maud can do that, why can't she work?"

After a day of 'counseling' at the prison, Maud asked Joe if a prisoner up for parole could live with her in the apartment in Joe's house. An argument ensued as Joe yelled, "No criminal is going to live in my house." She countered with, "But it's the will of the Lord." In the end, Joe won the argument, but Maud was not done with her conniving. She had a plan.

A few days later Joe had the day off from work and was watching a football game on television. This day would become yet another turning point in his life. Carla was at work, and Maud was occupying the in-law apartment. The New England Patriots were playing and Joe was engrossed in the game while relaxing in his living room.

As he was relaxing in front of the television, the doorbell rang. Joe wasn't expecting anyone. He thought that it was probably a salesman, or maybe the Jehovah Witnesses on their rounds. A little annoyed that his relaxation was being interrupted, his curiosity took over as he walked to his front door and opened it. Standing in front of him were two uniformed police officers. "Are you Joe Parker?" Wondering why they were asking, Joe answered, "Yeah, what's this about." The officer replied, " We've received a report from your mother-in-law that you hit her. Is that true?" Immediately, Joe's anger started to boil over. He was no longer trying to keep one ear on the football game blaring from the TV in the room behind him. "Hell no!" is all he said. Both policemen were watching his hands carefully. One officer kept his hands on his waist belt in case he needed to react quickly and draw his weapon. They both watched for Joe's reaction.

"You're welcome to come in and look around", Joe said, trying to show the officers that he had nothing to hide. "Show us your hands" one officer replied. Joe put his hands out in front of him about chest high and flipped them over a few times. The officers were looking for wounds and bruises that would show evidence that Joe had struck something, or someone. Joe kept his composure for the officers, but inside he was steaming with anger.

Maud took out a restraining order on you. She claimed you hit her", an officer explained. "This means you have to leave your house. Right now." As the message began to sink in, Joe's mind started to reel. The officers allowed him to get his car keys and grab a jacket, but that was all. They followed him through the house as he collected them.

Joe left and drove to a friend's house. From there he phoned Carla to tell her what had happened, what her mother had done to him. He ranted that Maud had lied to the police and had now taken over their home. For the next few days, Joe stewed in his anger while living at his friend's house.

CHAPTER 9

Carla came by to take the car because she needed it to get to and from her job. Being in the auto industry, Joe quickly found an old Volvo with a quarter million miles on it at a dealer auction. It was all he could afford.

Joe was determined not to lose the right to live in his own house. At least not without a fight. Since the restraining order had already restricted him from returning to his house, he filed a motion to plead his case. He had not assaulted Carla's mother, and he wanted his home back. He just wanted to be with his wife and family, and to live in peace again. Only the court could grant him his rights.

CHAPTER 10

On the day of the hearing, Joe arrived early at the courthouse. As he wandered the halls, he contemplated what he would tell the judge. He knew the judge would scrutinize every word he said. He didn't have money to hire a lawyer, so he'd be completely on his own. His future was in jeopardy, and was being threatened by a deceitful, manipulating con-artist. To regain his own home he knew he had to be articulate and convincing in front of the judge. It was his only chance, and he was super nervous.

A few minutes after he arrived, he sighted Maud entering the building. Accompanying her was a big, intimidating guy. He had long hair and a week's worth of stubble. With an angry look on his face, people moved out of his way as his stare focused on Joe. To Joe, it seemed obvious that Maud brought this goon along to intimidate him.

This massive guy was already known in the local community as a thug. Rocco Morelli was his name. As a member of a notorious motorcycle gang, he had been suspected of a number of crimes and was no stranger to the court system.

Rocco spotted Joe and walked up to him and put his chest to Joe's chin. He was much bigger than Joe, yet before Rocco could open his mouth, Joe said, "Get out of my way. I'm not afraid of you. I've tangled with bigger jerks than you." Not expecting this from Joe, Rocco stepped aside and let him pass into the courtroom. Joe's façade of bravery worked, but he was shaking in his boots with fear. Rocco could have easily crushed him if the confrontation had come to blows, and Joe knew it.

When court was in session and their case was announced, the magistrate called his mother-in-law's name several times for her to appear. His calls were followed by silence. Joe waited quietly, hoping that he'd win his case if she remained absent. No such luck. The magistrate looked at Joe and asked, "Is she here?" Joe reluctantly answered, "Yeah, I saw her in the hall with Rocco Morelli." The magistrate's eyes squinted as he exclaimed, " Oh, Rocco is here today." He was well know in this courthouse.

Hoping that it would help his case, Joe went on to explain that, "Morelli tried to block me from entering the courtroom."

CHAPTER 10

Just then, Maud sauntered into courtroom. She had a big grin on her face as she walked through the door with Rocco.

Joe had his turn explaining his side of the story to the judge, but the decision went against him anyway. The restraining order was not lifted. In the end, Maud's diabolical scheme worked. She won the right to live in his house, and he lost the right to live in his own house.

Joe was devastated. He had worked hard all his life. He had a wife, a family and a home. Now it was all pulled out from under him. All for trying to be compassionate and allow his mother-in-law to live with them and keep her comfortable until cancer took her. Instead, she took everything from Joe.

In his grief, Joe asked himself, "Where is my guardian angel now? Where is the spirit who had watched over me? Where is the guardian angle who had sent me the twenty dollar bill when I was hungry?" He thought to himself *It just isn't fair. What did I do to deserve this?*

Joe was so distraught that he filled the old Volvo with gas and headed south to Florida. He had to get away, far away, and as fast as he could. Florida offered familiarity, comfort, warm weather, and a chance at another new start. He had an old friend in Florida who would let him sleep on the couch until he got settled. He arrived about 30 hours later.

CHAPTER 11

As soon as he arrived in Florida he looked for a job. Before he could find one, his money ran out. And so did the patience of his host. Feeling he had overstayed his welcome, he decided to drive to the other side of Florida and try to find employment. He had worked for a car dealership there years before. Maybe he could get his old job back. The Volvo was in disrepair, but the drive was only a few hours. He filled the tank one evening and headed out.

His life to this point had a pattern of ups and downs, success followed by failure, followed again by success. The lows were low and the highs were high. He was never able to sustain middle ground for more than a few years at a time. Right now he was living again in one of the low points.

It wasn't more than an hour or so of driving when he began to smell something. It smelled like burning oil, and smoke was wafting into the cab of his car.

All of a sudden, the dashboard lit up with flashing lights and warning indicators. The car was overheating. Something was wrong.

Joe pulled off the highway just as the engine died. He had enough momentum to glide the old Volvo into a truck stop just off the exit. Rows of semitrailers were diagonally parked in the lot in front of a small restaurant. There was a maintenance garage to one side of the parking lot. A mechanic was busy at work and looked like a headless torso. His head was bent forward and hidden under a corner of the engine cowl.

Joe wandered unnoticed past the truckers and maintenance crew into the café. There was nothing unusual about a hungry traveler stopping in for something to eat. He blended in with the other patrons and no one paid him undue attention.

The smell of food augmented his hunger. After his last meal with his friend he had quietly slipped out of view and out of the house. He hadn't had anything to east since breakfast. A search of his pockets didn't turn up more than a few silver coins. Not enough for even a bag of potato chips.

While taking inventory of his surroundings, he spotted a sign over a door that pointed to the room down the hall. It was a chapel. Truckers were often on the road, away from home for several days at a stretch. The chapel was there for their spiritual solace on days when they were far from home.

CHAPTER 11

Trying to appear nonchalant, Joe sauntered past a table of truckers and slipped through the door under the 'Chapel' sign and into the sanctuary. At the far end of the room was a small statue of Christ on a pedestal. In the middle of the room there were three rows of church pews that appeared to have been salvaged from an old house of worship. Perhaps they were destined for the landfill, but salvaged instead to be used to provide a respite for lonely travelers. To Joe, they seemed like a convenient, out-of-sight refuge where he could spend the night.

As Joe sat in the chapel, he reflected on his situation, "What have I done to deserve this? I'm homeless, I have no money, and I don't know what to do. How did my life come to this?" As he sat alone with his head in his hands, tears rolled down his cheeks.

At first, he didn't notice the two long-haul truckers who had stepped into the back of the chapel, but they noticed him. This truck stop was on their weekly route and they routinely visited the chapel to help them maintain their spiritual commitment while away from home.

The site of Joe stopped them in their tracks. Before them was a young man who was clearly down on his luck. His misery was written on his face by the tears on his cheeks. The truckers walked up to Joe, and as one put a hand on Joe's shoulder, he asked, "What's wrong brother? Can we buy you a meal?"

Emotionally drained, Joe readily accepted. The two truckers escorted Joe back to the cafeteria where they sat down. As the waitress was pouring their coffees, Joe began to explain his predicament. "I left everything, including my family, back in Massachusetts. My car broke down and I have no money. I just want to get to Naples. I have a job interview lined up. It's my only hope."

In their travels, the two truckers had heard all sorts stories from people who claimed to be down on their luck. Yet there was a sincerity in Joe that touched their hearts. In their own lives, they had also experienced both good times and bad. "We can get you there. We're heading south tonight, but we can put out a call for truckers who are going in your direction. Come with us and we'll set you up."

Joe's upbringing afforded him good skills at sizing people up. There were no caution flags raised in his interaction with his newly found friends. He accepted their offer.

After the three consumed a hearty breakfast, they walked out of the cafe to the eighteen wheel rig in the parking lot. It was sitting empty, in a corner of the lot, with its engine chugging and the smell of diesel fumes in the air.

Joe sat in a seat behind the driver. The two truckers sat up front as they headed south on the interstate. Behind the cab was forty feet of trailer with a heavy cargo. Joe could feel its weight whenever the driver stepped on the brakes.

CHAPTER 11

As they drove, they listened to the CB radio squawking snippets of conversations between their brethren truckers on the road. The driver sitting in front of Joe picked up the microphone and spoke into it. "Are any of you heading west? We have a brother riding with us who is down on his luck and he needs a ride to Naples. Can anyone help him out?"

Within seconds an answer blared from the speaker on the CB radio, "I'm heading that way and would be glad to help. I'll be at the truck stop in an hour. I can pick him up there."

By the next morning Joe was where he needed to be, in Naples, on the west coast of Florida. He wasn't far from the home where he had once lived. The familiarity of his surroundings quenched his depression. His mood began to change. He felt upbeat and confident that he could start over, find work, and put the past out of his mind. Joe set out to get the job he knows well. Selling cars at a dealership.

Joe's life began to take shape again after he successfully landed the job he wanted. A small dealership hired him as their sales manager. Being a talented salesman, it didn't take long for him to earn a good paycheck. Several months passed and he bought a small house nearby and settled into his new existence. He felt Mem's presence and thanked her for looking after him.

His roller-coaster life was once again finding new heights. Yet paying the bills for his properties in both Florida and Massachusetts was not something he could easily afford. By selling the house in Massachusetts he could balance his finances, and at the same time exact some sweet revenge on Maud. It might also convince Carla to move south and join him and be a family again.

A few months later, he had a buyer for his Massachusetts home. The plan worked. Carla and the kids moved in with him in Florida, and Maud was evicted by the new owners. He was finally free of her. Once again, he had his life back.

CHAPTER 12

Life had settled into a quiet routine until one day when he received a phone call. Joe was at his home when Brian Parker called him. Brian had been married to Joe's mother, but they had divorced a few months before Joe was born. Brian was listed on Joe's birth certificate as being his father. In the conversation, Brian told Joe, "I'm not your father."

To Joe, this was just another slap to his face, another episode in a life long string of let downs. It seemed that every positive turn in his life, every light of hope would somehow be snuffed out by something or someone. Along the way, he had learned to never get too close to anyone, as it always seemed to end in pain and disappointment. The call from Brian Parker just was one more example. One more reason to maintain an emotional barrier between himself and others.

The revelation from Parker began to gel with the suspicions Joe had about his uncle Carrigan. The birth mark, the physical resemblance to Carrigan and the other circumstances now started to make sense. Maybe Carrigan was his real father.

Several weeks later, Joe returned to Massachusetts to visit his Mom who was in a mental health facility. In spite of her woes, she was still his mother and the only remaining family he had. During his visit, a life-long friend of hers showed him an advertisement in the personal section of the local newspaper. The heading on the ad read *"Looking for Joseph Michael Parker."*

Joe's middle name is Michael, but he wasn't sure if he was the one referred to in the paper. Even in the small community in north central Massachusetts, the odds of someone sharing his name were greater than zero. At first he ignored it, but his curiosity took control. Joe called the number given in the ad. A familiar voice answered the phone. It was his uncle, Dicky Carrigan. He said he wanted to talk, but face-to-face, not on the phone. Albeit a bit apprehensive, Joe agreed to meet him at a local bar.

It had been many years since they last met, but Joe recognized him immediately. Carrigan's resemblance to himself once again raised his suspicions about the man. Was he really his uncle, or something else? Could he be his real father?

It didn't take long for Carrigan to confirm it. A few minutes after they sat down together, Carrigan looked Joe in the eyes and admitted, "I'm your father." With those words hanging in the air, he waited

CHAPTER 12

for a reaction from Joe. Joe just looked at him, through him, and around him. Even though he had pretty much figured out that Carrigan was his father, there was no joy in the moment. Now he knew for certain who had almost beat his mother to death, abandoned him as a child, and left him to fend for himself. Joe controlled his anger long enough to listen to the rest of what Carrigan had to say.

Carrigan played his usual tricks while Joe watched and listened to him as they sat at the bar. Joe asked him if he had a cigarette. Carrigan looked around and spotted a pack of Marlboros on the bar in front of the man sitting on his other side. Carrigan nudged the guy with his elbow and pointed to a bar maid and said, "check her out". When the guy looked toward the gal, Carrigan snatched the pack of cigarettes and put it in his shirt pocket. He then turned to Joe, pulled out the pack and handed him a smoke.

A few minutes later, Joe noticed the guy next to Carrigan looking all around and his seat. He then went to the men's room, came back and continued to look around. Carrigan watched him for a minute and then asked, "What are you looking for?" He replied, "A pack of cigarettes." Carrigan offered, "Here, take one of mine." As he handed the guy a cigarette from the pack he had stolen.

This was typical behavior by Carrigan. Still making trouble wherever he went. Sometimes it would spark a fist fight, other times he was just a nuisance.

Joe was not amused and said, "I've seen enough. Have a good life." He got up and took a few steps toward the door. As he walked away, Carrigan yelled out, "You have a brother."

Joe kept walking and left Carrigan at the bar. He was disgusted with this person who claimed to be his father. He did believe him, however he still had seeds of doubt in his mind that made him wonder. In Joe's thoughts *this guy has lied to me before. Why is he telling me now that I have a brother?* Joe wasn't sure if he heard him right anyway. The distance and the noise in the bar distorted the words.

He wrote it off as just another lie. Joe went back to Florida and never saw Carrigan again.

CHAPTER 13

A few years flowed by. His job provided an adequate living and he loved the warm Florida weather. Family life had settled into a comfortable routine. As in any marriage there were occasional conflicts and disagreements. One day a disagreement developed into a heated argument with Carla. As she had done once before, she thrust a dagger through his heart with, "I'm having an affair. These children are not yours." Those words proved to be too painful for Joe to forgive. Like many marriages, theirs ended in divorce.

Even after her infidelity, untruthfulness, and disrespect of Joe, the court still favored her. The judge awarded everything to his former wife: the house, the bank accounts and the rest of their assets. To Joe it didn't seem fair, but it didn't surprise him. His past experience with the court system had taught him not to expect fairness. For the second time in his life, he is kicked-out of his own house. Joe is forced to leave.

It's familiar territory for him. His life has been replete with losses. One loss followed by another loss. He decided to quit his job and move back to familiar territory, Massachusetts.

Without a job, Joe knew that Carla would not be able to keep up with the bills and taxes on the house. Having no desire to find a job, she started to sell all of the possessions in the house. Furniture, clothing and everything else she could find ended up in yard sales. It wasn't long before she was forced to sell the house and move back to Massachusetts and move in with her family, kids and all.

If there was one positive aspect to his ex-wife and children coming north was that he got to see his kids. The children he helped raise were a source of great pride. He cherished them both. Even with doubts about their biological ties, his love for them never waned. He was committed to providing them with the emotional support and male influence. Joe wanted to be that fatherly role model even if he lived separately, and even if they weren't his biological offspring.

On Father's day, Joe was feeling down until his youngest son called him on the phone to say "Happy Father's Day." He wanted to see his Dad and go out to dinner. A nice father and son meeting was just the medicine Joe needed to lift him out of his funk.

CHAPTER 13

On the phone, Joe told his son, "I'll swing by and pick you up." His son replied, "Let's meet somewhere else, Mom's boyfriend is here." Joe replied, "So what? We are divorced. Your mom has a right to have a boyfriend." After a moment of tense silence, his son tells Joe, "It's your old friend Paul."

Joe's mind started to search for any Pauls that he knew who were old friends. There were two who came to mind. One owns a heating and cooling company, but he's gay. When he came out of the closet, his wife divorced him. He's not likely to be the same Paul whom Carla is dating.

The only other Paul Joe knows is his life-long best friend, but he lives in Florida. Joe's thoughts start to churn. Why is his son trying to keep him away from this Paul? Is this actually the Paul he knew in Florida? What is he doing up here in Massachusetts? Was Carla secretly having an affair with Paul while they were still married in Florida? Because of her admitted affairs, his suspicion is aroused, and his anger starts to seethe.

Before jumping to conclusions, Joe hit the speed-dial on his cell phone and called the Florida number for Paul. After a few rings, Paul answered the phone. Not wanting to sound like he's probing for information, Joe cagily engages Paul in small talk about Father's Day. "How is your day going? Have you seen your kids today?" Paul, just as cagily replies, "I'm with them now here in Florida."

Hearing a female voice in the background, which sounded very much like Carla, Joe asked, "Who is that with you?" Paul, stutters back, "That's my sister?" Joe asks, "What is she doing in Florida?"

Paul realized that Joe's probing questions are going to expose the truth. He admits to Joe, "I'm not in Florida, I'm up here in Massachusetts, and it's not my sister." Smelling a rat, Joe yells, "Why didn't you tell me you are seeing my wife?" Paul tried to calm him down with, "I didn't want this to hurt our friendship."

This is too much for Joe to take. His ex-wife is seeing his best friend. He wonders, *how long has this been going on*? Paul's revelation pushes Joe's anger to uncontrollable limits. Carla cheated on him during their marriage, and now his best friend is sneaking around with his former wife.

Emotions trump Joe's logic. He knows his ex-wife and Paul can do whatever they want, but he feels betrayed, and by both of them. His thoughts begin to turn wild with anger. *Was it Paul she was having an affair with all this time? Could Paul be the father of one of his children?*

His anger stewed for a few days. He can't get the rage out of his being, and it boils over. His fury contorts into a plan for revenge. One side of him says, "Don't do it." The other side screams, "He's going to pay for this!"

When Joe lived in Florida, he owned a shotgun. The tactical type of shotgun designed for people to

CHAPTER 13

use for home protection. It was black and had a short barrel. Not a weapon that was designed for hunting. He acquired it by legal means while in Florida, but in Massachusetts he did not posses the necessary documents for legal ownership. Joe's uncle could rightfully own it, so Joe asked him to hold it for him after he returned to Massachusetts.

With Joe's rage commandeering his judgment, he visited his uncle to retrieve the firearm. "A state trooper friend of mine wants to buy it," he told his uncle. Having no reason to doubt his story, his uncle gave the gun back to Joe with a half full box of ammunition.

Joe's anger was out of control and he knew it. Having lost everything to Carla in the divorce, and now this. He was beside himself with rage. He drove around with the gun in his car as he contemplated taking revenge on his former best friend, Paul. All the while, his emotions struggled with his conscience. He wanted no less than death for Paul, but he knew it was wrong. He knew it would end his own freedom, or worse.

In a moment of reflection and sanity, he reached out for help. He wanted someone to stop him. He called the police. At first the police thought it might be crank phone call, but Joe persisted. He begged them to intercede and stop him from what he was planning to do. "I'm gonna kill the bastard. I'm gonna blow his fucking brains out unless you stop me first. I need you to stop me." His conscience and anger were tugging at each other. For now his conscience was winning.

As he was driving around town, he passed a parked police car. The officer was using radar to clock motorists. Joe passed right by, hoping to be pulled over. The traffic officer ignored him and tended to his job of catching speeders. This just made Joe angrier. Now he felt betrayed, even by the cops. With his rage multiplying, Joe pulled into a parking lot and stopped his car. He sat there talking out loud to himself, and trying to calm himself down. For twenty minutes he tried to control his emotions.

His soul still pleading for help, he made a second call to the police station. "This is no joke. You'll be scraping this fucking guy's brains off the sidewalk if you don't stop me." In a moment of sane reflection he asks himself," What am I doing? I'm planning to kill my best friend." The gun he planned to use was loaded and lying behind him on the back seat.

Still sitting in his car in a parking lot, Joe continued to reflect on what he's doing. Yet his emotions were hard to control. All the pressures of his past had come together and have fallen upon him today. While he was trying to calm himself down, a van slowly drove by the driver's side of his car. The van driver glanced at Joe for a second as he passed by.

Cars continue moving past him. The same van crept by again and the driver gave Joe a surly stare. They caught each others glare as Joe mouths, "This is the wrong day to be fucking with me mister." At

CHAPTER 13

that, the van speeds up and disappeared behind some parked cars.

Within seconds, Joe's car was surrounded by squad cars and officers. Armed police dressed in tactical gear pointed guns at him. Before he had time to react, he was yanked from the car and thrown face down on the pavement. Several officers pounced on him and handcuffed him. Oddly, Joe is relieved by the treatment. Someone has saved him. His former best friend will live beyond the day.

He's placed in a squad car and driven to the police station. While there, he is placed in an interrogation room and told to, "Sit down and shut up." He's left alone, handcuffed to the bench and quietly follows orders.

Twenty minutes later, the door swings open and two officers walk in. They take seats opposite Joe with the table between him and them. They immediately start playing good cop, bad cop. "You're in a lot of trouble son. You could get jail time for this." The other cop interjects, "Let's give him a chance to explain himself. Joe, what is going on?"

Having had time to calm down, and thankful that he hadn't hurt anyone, Joe told them the story. His best friend is sneaking around behind his back and sleeping with his ex-wife. The one 'bad cop' softens his tone and asks for Paul's phone number. They weren't going to believe Joe's word until they verified his story. As far as they knew he may have already killed someone.

The officer dialed the number and put the call on speaker mode so everyone in the room can hear the conversation. He cautions Joe to, "Keep your mouth shut."

Paul answers, "Hi this is Paul." Paul hears, "This is officer, Mckinley, at the police department. Do you know a Joe Parker?" "Yeah, he's a good friend." The officers asks, "How long have you known him, and why would Joe have a loaded shotgun in his car with your name on one of the cartridges?"

Paul chuckles at Mckinley's statement. Mckinley tells him, "This is no laughing matter, Paul. Do you have a girlfriend?" Paul stops laughing and answers, "Yeah, she's Joe's ex-wife." The officer responds, "Now we're getting somewhere. Now you can see why he is so pissed off. No joke Paul, your life might have ended today. If you were fucking my ex-wife, you'd already be dead, and I'd get away with it being a cop. My advice to you is to get a restraining order against Parker." Again, Paul laughs it off, "I'm not afraid." Officer Mckinley tells him, "You're an idiot." And he hangs up the phone.

Still cuffed to the bench Joe sat quietly and listened. Mckinley looks at him and says, "I've been a cop for 19 years and most of that time a sergeant." With his head bent forward, he rubs his eyes and continues, "Most of the people who sit on that bench with a similar story are full of shit. They are the stupid person in the duo. I can count on one hand the times I have felt sympathy for the one sit-

CHAPTER 13

ting there. This is one of those times. If you had gone through with your plan and shot Paul, it would be considered a crime of passion. You might have gotten probation, or at least a light sentence. You would have gotten away with it."

Even though the officers are sympathetic, they aren't going to let Joe just walk out. "You haven't committed a serious crime, but an argument could be made for a charge of criminal threatening." The policeman went on to say that, "You stated your intentions to the police, but I understand that you never threatened Paul, so you didn't actually commit that crime." The police did not pursue a firearms charge either.

Still not willing to release Joe on his own recognizance, he was taken to a facility for a mental evaluation and a cooling-off period. The Henry Hayward Hospital in Gardner Massachusetts would be his home for the next few days.

The hospital reminded him of the facility where his mom resides. It's full of people whose shortcomings are quite obvious. He can see it in their blank stares and the incoherent sentences they string together, or when they have a conversation with a couch. It doesn't take Joe long to decide that he doesn't belong there.

After a day or two his anger had subsided. He is calm enough to approach a nurse and say, "When can I get out of here? I don't belong here." The nurse smiles, but doesn't answer. Joe tells himself *they probably hear this from everyone.* Not giving up, Joe tells every staff member he sees that he wants to leave. He tells anyone who would listen that he wanted a different type of help. This is not what he had in mind when he asked the police to stop him from committing a crime. He insisted that he'd, "Rather be in jail."

Late one afternoon, a few days after he was committed to the hospital, a woman approached him. She said to Joe, "I understand that you don't think you should be here." Joe answers, "Yes. Who are you?" "I'm someone who can help you", the woman responds with a smile. "I'm Dr. Lambert, and I may be able to release you."

Joe had been under observation ever since he arrived. Joe was not aware of it, but his moods and interactions with other patients were being monitored. The staff saw that he wasn't a threat to himself or others, but Dr. Lambert wanted a closer look before she released him.

She asked Joe to follow her down the hall and through the door marked 'Sensory Room'. The room was furnished as though it was someone's living room. A light was hanging from the ceiling in the center, and hidden speakers were lightly playing the sound of birds chirping. Joe walked in, took a seat on the recliner, put his feet up and exclaimed, "Are you kidding me? What is this room all about?" He's half amused and half annoyed that he is being patronized.

CHAPTER 13

Dr. Lambert explains that, "This is just a quiet place to talk. I want to hear all about why you are here?"

Joe has had plenty of time to think about the events of the past few days. His rage has died-out and he's reflective in his thoughts. As he sits there, he calmly tells the story to Dr. Lambert. The manner in which he questions his own emotions, and the fact that he credits the police for rescuing him from committing a terrible crime, all give Dr. Lambert reason to believe that Joe is sane and retrospective.

Dr. Lambert invites in Officer Mckinley, who was waiting in the hallway. Dr. Lambert now asks the officer to corroborate the events of that infamous day. Albeit from a different vantage point, his story matches Joe's exactly.

The next day, Joe is summoned to a room where a panel of social workers and doctors are already assembled. While they all sat in a circle of chairs, Joe told his story once again. After listening to Joe, a doctor says, "We think you are ready to be released, but we'd rather you stay for a few more days." Joe thinks about this offer for a moment and replies, "I'd consider it if you'd let me smoke. You took away my cigarettes and I could use one right now." With that, Joe was given a pack of cigarettes and he agreed to stay for a few more days. Other than the company, the accommodations weren't bad and the meals were free.

A few days later, still convinced that he's the only sane patient there, he is cleared to be released. But first, he had to go to court and appear before a judge. It was the final step before he would be granted his freedom. The judge asked him one question, "What are you going to do if I release you?" Joe was quick to respond. He had already made up his mind that, "I'm gonna sell everything and go back to Florida." They both knew that the best place for Joe was to be somewhere far away from Massachusetts. If he lost control of his emotions a second time, there's a good chance that he'd hurt someone.

While in the hospital, the events of the past few days had driven his desire to get far away. He wanted to be away from the people who always seemed to stab him in the back: his ex-wife, his 'best friend'. He had once made a home in Florida and yearned for those good memories to repeat. Massachusetts was no longer his comfort zone. Once again, he found himself alone and in search of meaning, happiness and stability. The same existence he'd been seeking ever since childhood.

The judge considered Joe's response for a moment and replied, "When you get there, go to the local sheriff's office and have him call me. Here's my phone number. I'll assure the sheriff that you are not a criminal, and that you've just had a bad day."

CHAPTER 14

A few days later, Joe packed all his worldly possessions in his car and began the drive back to Florida. After the divorce, the clothes on his back, and those in the back seat of his car were all that he had to show for all his years of work.

There was an old friend in Florida who agreed to let Joe stay with him for a few days. The familiar palm trees, white beaches and warm humid air greeted him when he arrived. Simply breathing the Florida air was enough to calm his nerves and bring to mind the better days he once knew there.

In Florida, his plan was to restart his career at the car dealership where he had once worked. When he arrived, his first-let down was that the car dealership was no longer in business. It didn't take him more than a few days before he had a job offer from a different dealership. The offer was for a position for which he was over-qualified, and at a lower pay scale than what he was used to. His discontent was further augmented by the fact that his new boss would be someone who had once worked under him at the other dealership. Never one to let his pride get in the way, he accepted the job anyway.

For several months, Joe lived paycheck to paycheck and making barely enough money to survive on. Most of his old friends had left, his old employer no longer existed, so the Florida he once knew had changed. The good memories he hoped to revive did not materialize. His job became drudgery and he slowly lost the motivation to succeed.

His whole life he had lived the quintessential life-of-hard-knocks. He was born with nothing, and given nothing growing up. He worked hard to make something of himself, only to have it taken away. A lesser person, a weaker soul might have long since given up. Again it was time for a change.

He wanted to get as far away as possible. To a place where he knew no one and no one knew him. With his tax returns, Joe had enough money to buy a one-way ticket to Hawaii. The postcard pictures of palm trees and sandy beaches were like those that had first attracted him to Florida. In Hawaii, he had no past, only a future. A future that he alone was in control of. His airline ticket took him to Honolulu, on the island of Oahu.

Oahu was true to the pictures and the lore. The beauty of the island was even more striking than the postcards. The mountains came straight up out

CHAPTER 14

of the ocean. Their slopes were a kaleidoscope of shapes and colors.

With little cash at hand, he found a room in a cheap hotel not far from Waikiki Beach. It was the beach pictured on that postcard. A long white beach with a sweeping curve from one end to the other. In the distance was the dormant volcano called Diamond Head, known to Hawaiians as Lēʻahi.

Aside from the natural beauty, the people lived up to their reputation. They were truly accepting and hospitable. Joe soon befriended a guy living in the same hotel, who had grown up in Hawaii. Joe came to know him as Mantis, although Scott was his real name. Their similar beliefs and circumstances drew them into long philosophical conversations. Both of their mothers had been diagnosed with schizophrenia. Mantis' philosophies on life and religion influenced and strengthened Joe's beliefs.

Their conversations often drifted toward their views on spirituality. They shared a belief that one's soul stays in existence long after the body dies. Mantis expressed his personal belief that humans are 'orbs' of energy. That 'orb' never dies. It takes on a new mission after it separates from flesh and blood. The 'orb' is one's soul and stays behind to guide those who are still living. That spirit looks after family and friends who are left behind in the world of the living. It watches over them until they all leave this world by death and they themselves become souls.

Joe recalled the day at the cemetery, when the cold wind plastered a twenty dollar bill to his face. How was that possible? He pondered what may have influenced him to call the police instead of taking revenge on his former best friend. What about the chance encounter that created the band SoulMine? It all made sense now. There were souls, guardian angels, who cared about him. Souls who nudged him in one direction or another. Souls who put the right thoughts in his head and even a soul who took care of his hunger. He felt that something, someone was watching over him. This was his religion.

While living at the hotel, Joe and Mantis would often talk, into the early morning hours, about their spiritual beliefs. They knew that many religions had conflicting ideas. Their followers were often so dedicated that they'd fight to the death to defend their particular religion. That in itself contradicted what their religion preached. Joe had learned from his work in the funeral business that no single religion was right for him, so from his observations and life experiences he developed his own religious theories.

CHAPTER 15

After a few months, Joe found a studio apartment he could afford. It would be his home for the next two years. He and Mantis remained friends while Joe jumped from job to job. He leveraged his expertise in automobile sales at a local dealers, and used his people skills while working at hotels and at other odd jobs.

One of his jobs was selling Maui Jim sunglasses from a kiosk 200 yards from Waikiki Beach. With the kiosk being that far from the beach, Joe had to attract potential customers on their way to and from the sand. People typically don't come to the beach in search of sun glasses, so Joe had to apply his best sales practices. These sun glasses were designed to amplify detail, clarity and color, giving the wearer an enhanced view of the surroundings. Joe knew that his best chance at making a sale was to have someone try them on. Like in the car business, getting a potential customer to test drive a car is a crucial step toward closing the deal.

Both Joe and Mantis were working for the same resort in Honolulu. Hawaii's excellent surfing conditions is why many tourist are attracted to the islands. Mantis, having lived in Hawaii all his life, was an excellent surfer. He was so good that the resort hired him to offer surfing lessons to their guests. He was so popular that on most days his lessons were fully booked and even had a waiting list. This day was no exception.

Joe was manning the kiosk and was applying his best sales techniques to convince potential customers to 'test drive' his sun glasses. Late in the day a tourist approached him and asked, "Do you know if there are any openings in the surfing class today?" Joe knew that the lessons were all booked, but he also knew that not everyone shows up. The tourist explained that, "I'm flying home to Australia tomorrow and today is my last chance for a surfing lesson." Joe offered, "I'll go check with my friend, the surfing instructor. Sometimes there's a no-show. Maybe today is your lucky day." In the back of his mind he knew that just by helping someone they might return the favor by buying a pair of sunglasses. Joe instructed him to, "Stay near your beach blanket. If I'm not back in fifteen minutes, it means I haven't been able to find a spot for you in a class."

Joe ran down to the beach and spotted his friend, Mantis. Mantis told him that surfing lessons are

CHAPTER 15

booked solid and all of his students have checked in. It wasn't the news that Joe wanted to hear. He had made the attempt, but a better outcome would have helped him sell a pair of sunglasses.

While he was walking on the sand back to the kiosk, he spotted a woman taking pictures of her husband and three young children. Always on alert to make a sale, Joe stopped to watch and thinks to himself *If I can get the camera out of her hands and put a pair of sunglasses on her, maybe I can make a sale.* His best chance at making a sale was to get her to try on these glasses. He notices that the husband already is wearing a pair of Maui Jim sunglasses.

Joe doesn't usually have the opportunity to make a sales pitch on the beach. His 'office' is the kiosk about 200 yards away. The family had not planned to be there either.

Alan, the father of the family, had served several years in the US Marines. He was fortunate to have been stationed in the tropical paradise of Oahu Island. After having served his country, he returned to the mainland and established himself as a successful businessman. Like Joe, he had built himself a lucrative career as a salesman. He shared many of the skills that had helped Joe survive a life of challenges.

Not having seen Hawaii since 1992, Alan had always yearned to show his family its natural beauty and introduce them to the pleasant inhabitants. He'd show them where he lived and he himself could reminisce on the fond memories of a time that seemed so long ago.

When he was in Hawaii as a Marine, Alan lived in an apartment. While searching for a place to stay for a family vacation, he contacted his former landlord. His old home, the apartment building, had been changed to a bed and breakfast and there was room available. So in January, he booked a two week stay with his family. They would be there in April. He looked forward to seeing his former landlord who had always been very kind to Alan. He always had a soft spot in his heart for her for being so friendly.

Tragically, a few days before Alan and his family arrived in Oahu, his former landlord's husband passed away. Alan was saddened that his family would not get to meet his old friend. There was no need to change their vacation plans except that they'd adjust their schedule to include attending the funeral.

The B&B expected several guests to arrive during the days surrounding the tragic death, so they had to stay open. They had no desire to turn away those who had planned, months in advance, a lovely vacation in the tropical paradise. The grieving family felt that their deceased love-one would have wanted it that way.

Alan and his family arrived in Oahu as planned and settled into the B&B, his former home as a Marine. Shortly thereafter, they all went to the funeral to pay their respect to the deceased. There was a re-

CHAPTER 15

ception planned for after the service, but since his wife and children had no real connection to the deceased they decided not to attend. Instead, they'd go walk along Waikiki Beach. The trip to the beach was a spontaneous decision and not something that was on their agenda. If anything, it would be a nice distraction from the sadness of the day.

That day on the beach, the wind was blowing stronger than unusual, and the surf was high. The waves and the wind seemed to be pushing people toward the area where Joe was looking for Mantis. The beach was tightly packed with people lying on beach towels and sitting on lawn chairs.

As people watched, Joe decided to play the role of the hospitable Hawaiian and said to Alan's wife, "Mam, if you want to get in the picture, I'll take it for you." Always the salesman, he knew that they won't leave without their camera, and as long as it's in his hands, he'd have a captive audience. He'd have enough time to make his sales pitch.

At first, the mother of the family tried to ignore Joe's offer but her husband interrupted with, "Sure, that would be *wicked* cool." Their accent and the adjective *wicked* were familiar to Joe. *Wicked*, used this way is the vernacular in Massachusetts. It's the native language of Joe's home state. Hearing it in Hawaii, he suspects he has something in common with this family.

Joe asks, Alan, "Where are you guys from?" Alan answered, "A small town in central Massachusetts."

No kidding, Joe says, "I'm from a small town in central Massachusetts. What town are you from?" Alan answered, "You've probably never heard of it." Interjecting a little sarcasm, Joe replies," Try me." Alan is thinking *who is this guy and why all the questions,*yet he answers, "I'm from Lunenburg."

With that, Joe aims the camera at the family of five from Massachusetts and says, "Are you ready?" and instead of saying *say cheese*, he says, "Say Leominster." and snaps the picture. The family all look at one another as if to say did I hear him say Leominster? (Leominster and Lunenburg are neighboring towns.)

With even more sarcasm in his voice Joe says," Yeah, your right, I'm from Leominster and I've never heard of Lunenburg." With surprise in his voice, Alan asks, "You're from Leominster?"

To Joe, there's something familiar about Alan, but he can't put his finger on it. Alan and Joe are close to the same age, so they may share some past acquaintances. In search of some common ground he asks Alan his name. They both start asking each other, do you know this person or that person. Nothing seemed to stick.

As they talked, Alan's wife and kids had become distracted and had moved several yards down the beach. Alan looked around and saw that they'd moved on without him. In haste, Alan ends his conversation with Joe and turns around and walks toward his wife and kids, trying to catch up to them.

CHAPTER 15

As Alan is walking away, Joe still has the feeling that there is something about Alan, some familiarity yet to be discovered. Joe has a thought and yells to Alan, "Hey, do you know Dicky Carrigan?" The question stops Alan in his tracks. He turned back toward Joe with an angry look on his face. The people on blankets and lawn chairs have now taken notice of this exchange and watch as Alan charges back to where Joe is standing.

Joe and Alan are now nose-to-nose, and Alan is outwardly angry. Joe is thinking *why is he so mad and how do I calm this guy down*? Everyone around is watching and listening when, in an angry tone, Alan asks, "Who the fuck are you and how do you know my dead father?"

For a second, Joe is stunned by the question. He now understands, and no longer fears Alan's anger. Joe tingles all over as goose bumps appear on his body. He feels the hairs on the back of his neck stand up. In a split second, a thousand thoughts and memories slammed through his mind with visions of his youth. He recalled that day when he met Dicky Carrigan in the bar. He remembered the last words he heard from Carrigan, "You have a brother." In an instant, Joe revisited his belief in the afterlife; that the souls of the dead are still present.

By now, people on the beach are quietly transfixed and wondering how this confrontation will unfold. Some are thinking that there's going to be a fist fight between these two guys. All eyes are on the two men. People are watching and listening. While the two were staring eye-to-eye, something incredible began to happen. Joe slowly raised his glasses to his forehead. He stared Alan in the eyes and froze for a few seconds. Joe knew an incredible fact, but ponders how he is going to tell this guy. He sputters a few incoherent sounds before he says, "He's my father too."

The beach-goers are stunned. One person gasps, then another. Both Joe and Alan begin to realize what has just occurred. Here, on a beach, thousands of miles away from their birthplace, the two half-brothers meet for the first time. People around them are as awestruck as are the brothers. A woman jumps up and runs to the resort hotel. Another woman nearby starts to cry.

After a few seconds of disbelief, they realize that this is really happening. They embrace, and tears flow. They stand back and look at each other again. They accept that it has to be true. They each have just met their brother.

The sights and sounds around them disappear. Their senses focus on the person before them. They have so much to say to each other. So many questions to ask. A lifetime of experiences to share. After the initial shock diminishes, they walk together back toward the kiosk. Alan's wife and kids follow. Tears flow from everyone.

EPILOGUE

Word spread quickly on the island about the two half-brothers who met each other for the first time on Waikiki Beach. In a few days, the story began to appear in newspapers world-wide. The chance encounter captured the public eye. Alan and Joe were swept up into a whirlwind of media frenzy. They were even invited to appear on national television.

In the following months, the brothers shared stories about the parts of their lives that had been lost to circumstance. Alan's family helped Joe find pieces of the puzzle that had been missing throughout his life.

Joe was lucky to have had emerged from the foster care system as a productive member of society. His upbeat personality was contagious. His positive outlook managed to trounce the negative forces that befell him one after another. His wits and innate intelligence helped him survive the pitfalls in the foster care system that too often become newspaper headlines.

Even today, the 'system' is replete with stories of abuse or even the occasional death of a neglected child. State-run child care agencies are often understaffed and underfunded. In spite of their best intentions, case workers often become spread too thin. Joe was fortunate to have been resilient, and was determined to succeed. His ambition was sprinkled with enough raw luck to help guide his way.

His story is one that should inspire young people who are in the foster care system. Both the cared for and the caregivers may find lessons within.

ALSO BY STEVE COX

No Shirt, No Shoes, No Service: A Hitchhiking Memoir
If You Love Me, Take Me Now

Steve can be contacted at:
stevec1280@aol.com, or stevec1280@gmail.com

www.ingramcontent.com/pod-product-compliance
Lightning Source LLC
Chambersburg PA
CBHW050540300426
44113CB00012B/2204